BAKING
magic

Kate Shirazi

with Susannah Blake

BAKING
magic

PAVILION

First published in the United Kingdom in 2010 by
Pavilion Books
Old West London Magistrates Court
10 Southcombe Street
London, W14 0RA

An imprint of Anova Books Company Ltd

Commissioning editor: Emily Preece-Morrison
Cover design: Georgina Hewitt
Home economists: Kate Shirazi, Valerie Berry, Monaz Dumasia
Copy editors: Barbara Dixon, Caroline Curtis, Siobhan O'Connor, Kathy Steer
Food stylists: Wei Tang, Monaz Dumasia, Charlotte Barton
Prop stylists: Wei Tang, Emily Preece-Morrison, Charlotte Barton
Photographers: Charlotte Barton, Lara Holmes, Yuki Sugiura
Indexer: Patricia Hymans

ISBN 978-1-862058-89-7

A CIP catalogue record for this book is available from the British Library.

10 9 8 7 6 5 4 3 2 1

Reproduction by Dot Gradations Ltd, United Kingdom
Printed and bound by Toppan Leefung Printers Ltd, China

www.anovabooks.com

Contents

Introduction

There has been intensive research carried out on the healing power of baking...

Scientists, nutritionists and psychiatrists have all spent hours pondering the curative qualities of cake (possibly). Can cakes be classed as a "health food"? Probably not, but they cheer you up and make you smile. So that's good enough for me.

Bought cakes that come in boxes and sit on supermarket shelves hold fond memories of a childhood Saturday afternoon treat. We (three children) would pester Mum, and sometimes she would give in and a cake would be bought. When we got home, the family of five would stare at this *small* round foamy sponge with a red, red jam and whiter-than-white "cream" filling. Yumm-eeeee. The cake would be sliced with surgical precision by the appointed "cutter". It had to be fair. Each slice would be examined at length by me, my brother and my sister, in order to determine whether one slice was bigger and therefore "unfair". The you-cut-I-choose rule was enforced with a rod of iron. Once the cutter had performed their task, they had to stand back and wait for the agonizing choice by the siblings. This extended doling-out of the small cake to the greedy family simply served to add to the deliciousness of it all. Looking at one of those cakes now, I wonder how we managed to get five slices out of it.

Cake is a luxury and a treat, but that doesn't mean that baking has to be difficult, complicated or make you sweaty with anxiety. Cupcakes, muffins and cookies are particularly easy to produce. This is not me being all cocky because I make them all day, every day. I am a firm believer in the process being as enjoyable as the result. They really are easy. What is truly gratifying is that, when you present a plate of home baked goodies to your admiring audience, they will gasp and smile and tell you how clever you are – and will secretly be cursing you for your aesthetic culinary skills. Let them inwardly worry about their own baking shortfalls. Wallow in the smugness. Just don't let them know that they took five minutes to knock up and three to decorate. You see – baking cakes, muffins and cookies is good for you in a truly holistic way. You don't even need to eat the darlings to make yourself feel better.

Kate

www.cakeadoodledo.co.uk

The recipes

The recipes in this book are meant to bring you joy, not drive you to distraction. If a recipe says it is easy or low-faff, I mean it. It is. If I confess that it's a bit of a fiddle, it means that I have found it a bit of a fiddle – whether technically or because it took up time. There are recipes to suit those who can't be bothered to spend more than 10 minutes in the kitchen and for those who don't mind dedicating a rather extraordinarily great expanse of their life to a project like chocolate buns. There are, of course, loads of recipes that fall somewhere in between.

When I cook, I find it difficult to follow recipes exactly. Some people prefer to follow recipes to the letter, and others have a rather more "freestyle" approach, flinging in alternative ingredients, snorting and tutting over methods and timings. I'll be as thrilled by either approach towards this book. Add, subtract, alter and embellish – I think that's what recipes should be all about. Now, I'll stop being bossy (for a moment, anyway). ...

Wheat and gluten

Unfortunately, some people seem to inflate at a rate of knots at the merest hint of gluten. In fact, just the word spoken out loud is enough to send some people scuttling. There are, of course, several conditions such as coeliac and Crohn's disease where gluten and particularly wheat are not a good idea, and certainly not something to be made fun of. Does this mean no cake? No, sirree. Please refer to "healing power of cake" as mentioned before. You can get gluten-free flour and I have been known to rustle up the odd ("odd" being the operative word) creation. Having had several interesting and not altogether successful baking sessions, I decided to throw caution to the wind and dispense with flour altogether. Ground almonds. They are the way forward. You get a delicious sponge with none of the "What's this weird cake made out of?" element. Just a glorious moist and utterly delicious cake. See recipes on p.49. p.52 and p.95.

Oven tips

Now it may seem obvious, but try to use your common sense when you're baking.
Every oven is different and has its own special foibles. Some ovens cook slightly quicker,
some slightly slower. Some ovens have "hot patches" so you'll need to turn the tray to
prevent half your cakes or biscuits browning more than the other half. So, all ovens cook
differently, and I don't want to be responsible for your burnt or raw cakes. Cakes are
done if they are firm to the touch and a bit springy on top. You can also insert a cocktail
stick (toothpick) into the centre – if it comes out clean, the cake is done. Blackened
charcoal, not good. Neither is your finger disappearing into the centre goo of the cake as
you prod. Once you've baked one or two recipes from this book, you might find you always
have to cook your cakes or cookies for a minute more or a minute less. These recipes are
all tested to perfection – but they've obviously been tested in my oven, not yours, so please,
please let common sense prevail.

Storage

How long do cakes, cookies and muffins keep? It really depends on how you store them.
Real cakes and cookies go stale quicker than shop-bought ones. I reckon on a good four
or five days in a biscuit tin with a tight lid. I bet they don't hang around for that long
though.... Muffins are much, much better when they're freshly made, so you really,
honestly do have to eat them on the day you make them. Personally, I'm a little bit brutal
about these things – muffins are an indulgence, and where's the indulgent luxury in
something that's not at its absolute best? So go on, dig in and gobble them up as quickly
as you can!

A little note on making muffins

I'd like to pretend there's a huge amount of skill and talent involved in baking a batch of golden-brown, sweetly scented muffins – but I'm afraid I'd be lying. They are so unbelievably easy-peasy to make, pretty much anyone can do it – even self-professed failures in the kitchen. But there are a few secrets to making really light fluffy muffins that differ from cakes and cookies – see in particular point three below (which may well appeal directly to the more slapdash cooks among us).

Number 1: To make a sweeping generalisation – combine your dry ingredients, combine your wet ingredients, put the two together and bingo: 12 muffins!

But before you get to this stage, there's a golden rule...

Number 2: Even if this seems like a faff, do it anyway! Sift all your dry ingredients together before you add the wet ingredients. You want your flour, sugar, cocoa, etc. to be as light as air, filling your mixing bowl in soft drifts like freshly fallen snow.

Number 3: Once you add the wet ingredients, don't over-mix! The temptation will be to give the batter a good old beating to make sure you've got a lovely smooth mixture. But this is wrong, wrong, wrong. Give it a gentle, brief stir – just enough to combine the ingredients, but no more than that. The average muffin mixture will still look a bit lumpy and chunky, and if you've still got a few streaks of flour – don't worry about it. Just scoop up big spoonfuls of the mixture, dollop them into the cases, then bung the tray in the oven. Twenty minutes later you'll be in heaven and wondering why you don't make these gorgeous creations every morning.

And if you don't follow this advice? Well, they'll still be edible, but your muffins won't have that fabulously fluffy texture that all the best muffins should have. They'll be a little tough, a little bit more solid than you'd like. So take my advice and always give your muffins the quick 1-2-3 treatment.

A little note on melting chocolate

A word here is needed about melting chocolate. Some of the recipes require chocolate to be used in its heavenly liquid form. There are two methods of melting chocolate (three, if you count giving it to a child to hold in the back of a car).

The first is the safest! Place the chopped-up chocolate in a heatproof bowl over a saucepan of barely simmering water. The crucial thing here is that the bottom of the bowl must not touch the water; the chocolate gets too hot. Nightmare: grainy ghastly mess; straight in the bin; tears. Don't do it.

The second method is quicker, more gung-ho, and I like to think of it as the rapid-assault method of melting chocolate. Quick, brutal – but not without risk: the microwave. Put the chopped chocolate into a microwaveable container, then zap it. Do short bursts of only 10–15 seconds and stir between each zapping. I recommend you stop while there are still some lumps and just keep stirring – the residual heat will melt the rest. The danger here is going for the burn (especially with white chocolate): one second, it is fine and dandy and thoroughly enjoying its little warm-up; the next second, Whoa! All gone horribly, horribly wrong. Have you ever tasted burnt chocolate? Nasty.

Batches of cookies

Now we need to have a full and frank discussion about how many cookies each recipe makes. I'm getting all tense writing this, I'll have you know. Most recipe books have a little bit saying 'makes 24 cookies' or something similar. This book will not. Each recipe will make one batch – a do-able, edible batch. You shouldn't have so few as to to make it not worthwhile and you shouldn't have too many so you are eating them for weeks. The problem with stating numbers is that I positively *want* you to use different sorts of cutters. How the devil do you work out how many cookies would be made using a heart-shaped cutter, if someone decides to use a giant T-Rex cutter? If you roll the dough two more times than me, you'll have a thinner biscuit and you'll get more. Do you see my point? My small teaspoon is going to be different from your small teaspoon. Embrace the unknown, just make the cookies and enjoy them – don't let yourself get hung up on the fact that a recipe says 'makes 24' and you've got 12 – or 45.

Equipment

Top tips for getting yourself kitted out

In terms of kitchen equipment, you don't need anything complicated for baking. Just an oven, some scales, a measuring jug, some measuring spoons, a big bowl and a wooden spoon for mixing, a sieve for sifting, maybe a saucepan for melting or warming, possibly a fork for whisking up any liquid ingredients. And, of course, the right tins and pans. Don't kid yourself, the tins are really the only bits of kit you absolutely cannot do without, but it's an investment you won't regret.

Cupcake and muffin cases

For muffins and cupcakes you need a muffin pan and paper cases – I like to use cases for muffins as well as cupcakes as it makes the finished muffins look so much more appealing – and it'll make your washing up so much easier, plus there are the benefits of cases for muffin transportation should you wish to consume muffins outside the home. You can get plain old white papers cases in every supermarket, and many stock pretty patterned ones as well. But it's worth having a search in kitchen shops, too, because it's here that you'll find the best selection of colours and patterns to add a little bit of flair to your baking.

But what size of pan and papers? Muffin pans and cases come in a mind-boggling array of sizes and it would be fair to wonder – which ones should I use? As a general rule, I've used a medium-sized muffin pan for the recipes in this book. Which means the batter quantities are enough for 12 fantastic cupcakes or muffins. So, should you wish to use a muffin pan with larger cups, you'll just end up with fewer cakes, but they'll be a whole lot bigger – and you may need to bake them for a minute or two longer. The only really important thing is to place the cases in a muffin tray before you put the mixture in. So please take my blithe comments about how many cakes are produced by every recipe as a guide only.

A few of the recipes in this book use a mini muffin pan, so you get lots of little diddy muffins. But again, if you want to use one of the basic muffin mixtures and cook it in a mini muffin pan – go ahead and just reduce the cooking time accordingly. (You'll also need to halve the recipe quantities – unless you want to make a gazillion muffins!)

You can also find muffin pans in funky shapes. My favourite is the heart-shaped muffin pan, which produces the most gorgeously shaped muffins imaginable. Obviously it's a must for Valentine's Day, but your lover will also adore you for making them heart-shaped muffins any day of the year; a batch for your mother on Mother's Day will make her crumple with pleasure; a plateful for the girls just because they're girls... You see, the possibilities are endless!

Silicone lining

The one bit of kit I think is absolutely critical for the enjoment of your biscuit making experience is re-usable silicone linings. I cannot praise them highly enough and I really wouldn't even consider starting to make a biscuit without one on my baking sheet. They are washable and re-usable. I bought a roll of this magic stuff about three years ago and cut it to fit the size of my baking sheets. It's still in action. Sometimes a cursory wipe is even enough if I'm feeling particularly slovenly. *Nothing* sticks to it. Ever.

Piping bags

If you choose to undertake some piping, and I hope you do, may I make a suggestion? Buy a packet of parchment piping (decorating) bags. They are small, one-use wonders. Although I mention fine nozzles (tubes, or tips) quite a lot, you don't actually have to use them. By snipping the very end off the bag, you can achieve a fine line of piping. Nozzles give you a slightly more polished result, that's all. Again, these are available in kitchen and sugar-craft shops everywhere. If you do want to buy nozzles, you really only need three – a couple of fine ones for piping lines and patterns (size 2 and 4) and a chunky star-shaped nozzle for piping mountains of buttercream.

Top tip for filling a large piping bag: turn the edges down and sit it in a mug and it's really easy to plop in the icing without creating havoc. When filling a small piping bag, use a teaspoon, or a little palette knife to fill the bag. Only fill the bag a third full, other-wise, when you fold the top over, the icing squidges out all over your hands.

Ingredients

Top tips for getting yourself stocked up

If you are reading this, it is more than likely that you have a roof over your head and the ability to make a few choices about what you do and don't want to eat. Lucky you and lucky me, quite frankly. This isn't meant to be a lecture, but I do like the idea of making cakes and cookies with a conscience. If you are going be bothered to bake, bake with nice ingredients. I am not saying that everything has to be organic and grown within a 150-foot radius of your dwelling, but why not use good-quality cocoa (Green & Black's organic cocoa does make the best chocolate cake *ever*) or unwaxed lemons (who wants to eat a load of wax?). And please, please, *please*, use free-range eggs. If you'd seen my hens the day they had been rescued from the battery, you'd use free-range eggs, too. Phew. I think I'll just go and lie down on my organic fair-trade lavender-scented hemp mattress and chew on some fennel seeds ...

The ingredients in this book are pretty straightforward. Most of the stuff can be bought in the supermarket, but anything you can't get there can be found in a health food store. If you can't find decorative frivolities, there are lots of brilliant online shops, which will send you a parcel full of excitement (after you have paid them, of course). These places are also an Aladdin's cave for cookie cutters. Pop what you want into a search engine ('sugar craft suppliers' is a good start) and *voilà* – a cornucopia of delights.

Butter or margarine

Now on to some other ingredients' top tips. Strike me down and write an apoplectic letter to the newspaper if it makes you happy, but I really think cakes are better made with soft margarine rather than butter. There. I've said it. The world continues to turn and I do believe that the roof hasn't been struck by lightning. Most things are better with butter: pastry, cheese sauce, scones ... and I wouldn't want margarine melting onto my crumpet, thank you very much. I just feel that you get a more consistently light sponge with a soft margarine. It's up to you entirely and you'll see recipes for both, but using soft margarine means that you can bung all the ingredients into one bowl and whizz away. It can't get any easier. Cookies or biscuits, however, are better made with butter – preferably unsalted – and all the recipes here are based on this. Margarine will make them taste foul and the consistency will be wrong. Even that spreadable butter is no good – it's too soft – don't do it.

Chocolate

You have probably heard many times before that what you cook will be only as good as the ingredients you use. Silk purse, sow's ear and all that. I have to say that this is very relevant to these recipes, *but* – you are under no obligation to buy only the finest single estate 72% chocolate, harvested by a man called Eric. Yes, you get what you pay for, but buy what you can afford and whatever strikes you as the best choice at the time. I am sure that a pudding made with single estate chocolate will taste better than a pudding made with cheap chocolate. But unless you are comparing and contrasting the two puddings, the one made with cheap chocolate will still taste good. It just won't be ambrosial.

A serious point to consider when buying chocolate is the issue of Fair Trade. Now, I really don't want to rant and make you, dear reader, feel uncomfortable and guilty. We do need to be aware, however, that the business of chocolate is often the cause of hideous injustice for the cacao farmers. There are plenty of Fair Trade chocolate brands available now. These are not difficult to find, and I reckon that the chocolate really does taste better. The finish is generally smoother. Yes, they are more expensive. I am happy to pay the extra because I see chocolate as a treat, not an everyday food, and I'm not thrilled at the thought of the farmer being ripped off. Up to you.

Cocoa

The one ingredient I do get very bossy about is cocoa. Cocoa and drinking chocolate are not the same. If a recipe says cocoa – for goodness' sake, use it. If you use drinking chocolate, you will be adding dried milk powder, sugar, all sorts of weird fats, and salt – and the recipe will not work. The only thing you may substitute for cocoa powder (unsweetened cocoa) is finely grated 100% cacao, which is utterly fantastic.

The icing on the cake

Many of the cakes in this book are deliciously low-maintenance – in other words, low-faff. I have suggested two sorts of particularly good "low-faff" icing. The first is glacé icing made with water or lemon juice. It's a question of sieving the icing (confectioners') sugar, adding the liquid and stirring. That's it. The second icing is buttercream. Butter, sieved icing sugar. Stir (albeit quickly in a beating-type manner). Flavours, colours and embellishments may be added, but they are a doddle.

Even more of a doddle is plonking something on top a cake or muffin straight out of a jar or tub. Why not? Nutella, lemon curd, mascarpone, whipped double cream – all delicious and simply divine (darling) spread on top. I feel I should point out that low in faff doesn't actually mean low in cost. An Extremely Posh Rose Cupcake is really quite extravagant – those roses don't come cheap. Hey-ho. All worth it in the world of cupcake exquisiteness, I say.

For cakes that involve a bit more fiddling and twiddling and where you have to make some decorations in advance, fondant icing is the order of the day. Fondant icing is made with powdered icing sugar which generally has had some dried glycerine added to it. You need to get this in powder form. It is available in lots of supermarkets.

But, pay attention please! If you are looking in a bewildered manner at the shelves of the supermarket and you are wondering whether to buy anything that calls itself "rolled fondant", "ready-made frosting" or "ready to use royal icing" and generally comes in a tub, step away. If you are not sure, just buy a box of ordinary icing (confectioners') sugar and make glacé icing.

Colouring

You will see that I am partial to a drop of colour on my cake. I remember one woman wanting reassurance that the electric-blue cake that little Crispin was about to tuck into was entirely natural. I looked at the vivid blue and looked at her and had to break it to her that, in fact, there was nothing very natural about a food item that bright. Having said that, there are companies out there (Sugarflair for instance – available widely) who produce quite a range of tartrazine-free colours for those whose eyes start spinning and their skin forming a thin film of sweat when it comes to artificial colours – and that's just the parents waiting for their children to absorb the colour and go on a behaviour free fall. But think of the possibilities of harnessing the energy from a small child in the throes of a colour-induced frenzy of hyperactivity. I may have just solved one of the biggest eco-conundrums of our time. You see? Cakes! I tell you.

Back to colour, gels are much better than the liquid colourings. They don't thin the icing and the colours tend to be much more versatile. I love them. You can get them from good kitchen shops and sugarcraft specialists. Word of warning: a little goes a long way.

Glacé icing

This is the simplest and most useful icing. Minimum ingredients and minimum fuss. Very easily correctible if you make it too thick or too thin.

✳ Makes enough for 12 cupcakes

200 g/7 oz/1¼ cups icing
   (confectioners') sugar, sifted
juice of 1 large lemon OR
   55 ml/2 fl oz boiling water
gel food colouring of your choice

Put the sifted icing sugar in a bowl. Add the liquid slowly, a little at a time, and stir until smooth. Stop adding liquid when you like the look of the consistency. It should be a smidgen thicker than double (whipping) cream.

Add a tiny amount of colour – use a cocktail stick (toothpick) dipped into the colour. You can always add more if you want, but there is no way to undo a lurid amount of colour without making a super-huge batch of icing.

Royal icing

This is a great icing for piping. It's not that tricky, but you need to watch the consistency. An icing that hold peaks like a stiff meringue is what you need.

✳ Makes enough for 24 cupcakes

2 large free-range egg whites
500 g/1 lb 2 oz/about 3¼ cups
   icing (confectioners') sugar,
   sifted
2 tsp freshly squeezed lemon
   juice

Put everything into a large mixing bowl, and whisk away for 4–5 minutes until the mixture is very white and standing in stiff peaks. It should be really quite stiff. If the mixture is too cement-like, add a few drops of lemon juice or boiling water. If it is too runny, add a little more sifted icing sugar.

This makes a lot of icing, so you may wish to halve the quantity, but it does keep well for around a week in the refrigerator if you seal it really well. I put a layer of cling film (plastic wrap) on top of the surface, then seal in an airtight plastic container.

Buttercream

❋ Makes enough for 12 cupcakes

225 g/8 oz/1½ cups icing
(confectioners') sugar, sifted
100 g/3½ oz/scant ½ cup soft
unsalted butter
½ tsp vanilla essence (optional)

Beat everything together in a large bowl for a few minutes until light and fluffy. If the mixture looks a little on the heavy side, ½ teaspoon boiling water whisked in works wonders.

If you want coloured or flavoured buttercream, add away to your heart's content (see suggestions below).

Coffee

Add 1 teaspoon very, very, *very* strong espresso or filter coffee (made with instant coffee – 3 teaspoons coffee granules with just enough boiling water to make it liquid). Mix through thoroughly.

Chocolate

Add 2 teaspoons sifted cocoa powder to the buttercream mixture. If you want it more chocolatey, add more. If you are feeling very extravagant, melt 60g (2 oz) good-quality dark (at least 70% cocoa solids) chocolate in a bowl over a pan of simmering water, and add that, too. Mix through thoroughly.

Lemon

Add the grated zest of 1 unwaxed lemon and 2 teaspoons freshly squeezed lemon juice. Mix through thoroughly. This works well with lime, too. And orange, come to that.

Fondant icing

Fondant icing is the lovely, glossy, shiny basis for all the cakes' preliminary icing. You can buy boxes of fondant icing (confectioners') sugar in big supermarkets and some sugarcraft shops. We are talking about a powdered product here, *not* to be confused with solid blocks of sugar paste (sometimes called "rolled fondant"). Not the same thing at all.

175 g/6 oz/1½ cups fondant sugar
55ml/2 fl oz boiling water or lemon juice

As for glacé icing, just mix the ingredients together, but this time you want a really stiff, almost dough-like consistency. I put it in the mixer with the dough hook, much easier.

Place in the top of a double boiler, or in a bowl over a pan of barely simmering water. GENTLY heat. Don't let the water boil; if the fondant gets too hot, it loses its lovely shiny appearance. As it warms, it gets runnier.

If the fondant is getting warm and melting a bit, but is still very stiff, add a bit more liquid and stir until it looks a bit looser, like very thick cream.

I find it easier to take it off the heat at this stage and transport dollops into separate bowls to add colour. It will stiffen up again quite quickly, just add a few drops (literally) of water to loosen it up. The consistency you want to end up with is thick, thick soup. Actually, even cheese sauce-like! Lump-free, of course.

Happy hens, happy eggs

Now I know I've already talked about using "nice" ingredients, but I feel the need to harp on a little bit more on the issue of eggs. The vast majority of recipes in this book are going to call for at least one egg, if not two. And if you're taking this book seriously, you're going to be trying out a lot of recipes. Multiply that by one or two eggs for every batch of cakes or cookies you bake – and you will be buying a whole lot of eggs before your baking days are over.

When it comes to choosing eggs, it's really a no-brainer. They need to be free-range. The hens that laid the eggs should have been free to roam around outside, pecking about, looking for food, deciding what they fancy and snapping it up. They should have had enough space to open up their wings and have a good flap, and the opportunity of a hedge to scuttle under should the mood take them. They just need the basics, just like *you* expect the basics.

What they should not have been subjected to is being crammed into a cage that's not even big enough to turn around in, then condemned to a life of eating and laying, eating and laying. And, of course, once their production drops and they're past their prime, they should still be valued, they shouldn't just be discarded because it's taking them more than a day to produce an egg. I'm talking about battery farming here – it's not very nice, so please do avoid the eggs produced from battery-farmed hens because you're not helping anyone ... least of all the hens.

You can do your bit by purchasing only free-range eggs and products that use free-range eggs (that is egg sandwiches, cakes, cookies, mayonnaise, quiches, pasta...), and this book does a little bit more. For every copy sold, a donation is made to the Battery Hen Welfare Trust (BHWT). This wonderful organisation, which works in a constructive and positive way with the industry and those farmers producing battery-farmed eggs, aims to promote and ensure a happier, better life for the 20 million battery hens currently in cages. The BHWT's goal is to inspire us, the public, to do all we possibly can to achieve a better future for these hens – whether it's through our supermarket shopping, or by us adopting a battery hen (or six, see below) – and thus help farmers to consider and facilitate the options for change to produce and keep happier hens. Check out BHWT's website at *www.bhwt.org.uk* to find out more about what you can do to live in a world of happier, cluckier hens.

Raising your own

For the really hardened chicken welfarer, there's another exciting option. If you've got space and time, and your council allows the raising of hens in your area, you can adopt a hen from the BHWT and reap the reward not only of freshly laid eggs, produced with the aid of your good self, but also the pleasure of transforming a pale and balding bird that's not even quite sure how to peck or flap into a pecking, clucking, flapping, feathery brown hen that's as happy as any hen can be. And hens really do make surprisingly good pets – they're friendly, cheeky and, best of all, pretty low-maintenance. So check out hen houses and spacious runs and the options for adopting, and enjoy your egg-laying hens in the way they should be enjoyed ... through the medium of the cake!

cakes

Your basic no-mucking-around cupcake

This is the ultimate low-faff cupcake. Personally, I like to see a variety of sprinkles and sweets (candies), but I have a cupboard full of alternatives, which makes life easier. You can even choose from a great selection of sprinkly pots that have four different types of sprinkles in one pot. Enjoy. Incidentally, this sort of cake was a firm favourite with my all-time best ever hen, the very wonderful Jean.

*Makes about 12

110 g/4 oz/1 cup self-raising flour, sifted
110 g/4 oz/½ cup caster (superfine) sugar, sifted
110 g/4 oz/½ cup margarine, softened
1 tsp baking powder
2 large free-range eggs
1 tsp pure vanilla extract
1 quantity of glacé icing (p.17)
sweeties (candies) and sprinkles, to decorate

You will find these pictured on pages 26-27

TOP TIP:

Always sieve the flour and sugar – it doesn't take long and makes all the difference, believe me.

Preheat the oven to 160°C/325°F/Gas mark 3. Line a 12-hole muffin tin (pan) with cupcake cases (baking cups). Put all the ingredients (except the icing and sprinkles, of course) in a mixer (food processor, food mixer, or just a big bowl with an electric whisk). Mix really well until the mixture (batter) is light and fluffy.

Plonk heaped teaspoons of the mixture into the prepared cases, and bake in the oven for about 20 minutes until golden, and firm and springy when you give them a light prod on top. Let them cool before preparing the icing – on a wire rack if you want, but not 100 per cent necessary.

To make the icing, you really must sift the icing sugar. Add the water really slowly (a teaspoonful at a time), and stir until you have a consistency like thick double (whipping) cream. Pour a little icing on top of each cake, and add whatever decoration takes your fancy before the icing dries.

Buttercream mountain

This cupcake is exactly the same as the basic cupcake and the rather impressive mountainous swirl is simplicity itself. Should the idea of piping get you a bit hot and bothered, fret not. Just smear a thick layer of buttercream over the cake with a knife. It will still be wonderful.

✳ Makes about 12

110 g/4 oz/1 cup self-raising flour
110 g/4 oz/½ cup caster (superfine) sugar
110 g/4 oz/½ cup margarine, softened
1 tsp baking powder
2 large free-range eggs
1 tsp pure vanilla extract
1 quantity of buttercream (see p.18)
food colouring (optional)
sprinkles (optional), to decorate

✳ *You will need a large piping (decorating) bag with a star nozzle (tube)*

✳ VARIATION:
If you want to make lemon cupcakes, omit the vanilla extract and add the finely grated zest of a lemon.

Preheat the oven to 160°C/325°F/Gas mark 3. Line a 12-hole muffin tin (pan) with cupcake cases (baking cups). Sift the flour and sugar into a large mixing bowl, food processor or food mixer. Add the margarine, baking powder, eggs and vanilla, and beat until the mixture (batter) is really pale and fluffy. Plop heaped teaspoons of the mixture into the prepared cases, and bake in the oven for about 20 minutes until golden and firm to the touch.

While the cakes are in the oven, you can get on with the buttercream. Put the softened butter in a big bowl and sift in the icing (confectioners') sugar (don't try getting away with not sifting the sugar – I can almost guarantee you will be wailing over a horrid gritty, lumpy mixture). Beat the living daylights out of it all till it's lovely and light.

Add whatever flavouring you want – a few drops of vanilla or some lemon juice – and the merest dab of colour from the end of a cocktail stick (toothpick). If the mixture is a bit too stiff, add a teaspoon boiling water and beat away.

When the cakes are cool, put a star nozzle (tube) into a piping (decorating) bag. If you put the piping bag into a mug or tumbler, it is much easier to fill. Plonk the buttercream into the piping bag and swirl away. Gild the lily with sprinkles, sweeties (candies) or drizzles of syrupy sauces.

Your classic butterfly cake

Who doesn't love these cakes? They are easy-peasy, and I think look fantastic. You can go for completely plain butterfly cakes with unadorned buttercream, but that would be not quite in the spirit of this book. Colour the buttercream – oh, go on, you know you want to.

✳ Makes about 12

1 quantity of basic cupcakes
(see p.24)
1 quantity of buttercream
(see p.18)
gel food colouring of your choice
icing (confectioners') sugar for
dusting (optional)

✳ *You will find these pictured on pages 26-27.*

Have your cooked cupcakes at the ready. Decide how many colours you are going for, and divide the buttercream into the appropriate number of bowls. Tint the buttercream with tiny dabs of colour.

With a small, sharp knife, cut the central portion out of the top of the cake. I like to delve down a bit so that you end up with an almost conical-shaped lid. Set the "lids" aside. Plonk some buttercream into the hole left by your delving. You could pipe it in, but the extra washing up then means that this recipe may qualify for an extra faff point.

Cut each lid in half and "place delicately" (more plonking) on top of the buttercream in the manner of a butterfly about to fly off. For a bit of extra finesse, dust the tops of the cupcakes with icing sugar. Purely optional and, if you are in true low-faff mode, you certainly won't bother.

Basic extremely low-faff square cakes

Well, this is a right old humdinger. Later in the book it gets beautifully faffy, messing about with all sorts of complications. These little dollops are really easy. It's a tray bake. Sshhh. Don't tell anyone.

✳ Makes about 12 if you can be bothered to put them in cases (baking cups)

110 g/4 oz/1 cup self-raising flour
110g/4 oz/½ cup caster (superfine) sugar
110g/4 oz/½ cup margarine, softened
1 tsp baking powder
2 large free-range eggs
1 tsp pure vanilla extract
1 quantity of glacé icing (see p.17)
gel food colouring of your choice
sprinkles of your choice, to decorate

✳ *You will find these pictured on pages 26-27.*

Preheat the oven to 160°C/325°F/Gas mark 3. Grease and line a 20-cm/8-in square baking tin (pan).

Sift the flour and sugar into a large mixing bowl, food processor or mixer. Add the margarine, baking powder, eggs and vanilla. Turn on or beat like fury until it's all pale and fluffy. Tip the mixture (batter) into the prepared baking tin and level carefully. Bake in the centre of oven for about 20 minutes or until the cake is firm to the touch and golden. Cool on a wire rack.

Make the icing (see p.17). You now have two options here. For both options, you need to have the cake upside down so that the bottom of the cake is the part that's iced. If the top of the cake is not level, just level it by slicing the uneven bit off with a sharp knife so that the cake sits flat.

Option one means that you cover the whole cake in icing, add the sprinkles and cut into squares when the icing is dry. Place each square in an individual case (baking cup).

Option two involves cutting the cake into squares first, then drizzling the icing over the individual squares so that the icing dribbles down the sides of the cakes, too. Add the sprinkles and, when the icing is dry, place the squares in cases.

Carrot cupcakes with honey orange cream cheese frosting

There are so many recipes for carrot cake around that I'd say, if you have a favourite one, try it in cupcake cases (baking cups). This is my favourite – one of those recipes on a scrappy bit of paper tucked into my collection. I like the fact that the frosting contains no sugar, being sweetened with honey. One thing I would suggest – use only proper cream cheese – sometimes sold as curd cheese. I've never had much success with the white soft cheese sold in supermarkets everywhere. It's too runny.

✳ Makes about 10

175 g/6 oz/1 cup soft brown
   sugar
175 ml/6 fl oz sunflower oil
3 large free-range eggs
150 g/5 oz/1¼ cups plain
   (all-purpose) flour
1½ tsp bicarbonate of soda
   (baking soda)
1½ tsp baking powder
1 tsp ground cinnamon
½ tsp freshly grated nutmeg
pinch of salt
225 g/8 oz/1¼ cups grated or
   shredded carrot

For the cream cheese frosting
1 x 225 g/8 oz packet cream
   cheese (not soft or light cream
   cheese), softened
2 tsp honey (or more to taste)
grated zest of 1 unwaxed orange
orange sprinkles, to decorate

Preheat the oven to 180°C/350°F/Gas mark 4. Line a 12-hole muffin tin (pan) with cupcake cases (baking cups). Mix the sugar and oil in a large bowl. Add the eggs and mix well. Sift in the dry ingredients, and beat everything together until really well combined. Next add the grated carrots and stir through well.

Place spoonfuls of mixture (batter) in the prepared cases, and bake in the oven for 15–20 minutes. Watch these like a hawk, as they have a tendency to burn. If the tops are getting a bit dark and it looks like the innards are still raw, cover with greaseproof paper or baking parchment, and cook a little longer. Remove from the oven and allow to cool.

While they are cooling, make the frosting. Put the cream cheese in a bowl, and beat until softened. Stir in the honey and orange zest. Give it a taste to make sure it is sweet enough. Add a bit more honey if you want. When the cakes are cold, spread the frosting over the top and decorate at will.

Lemonylicious

I love lemony things. So do lots of other people, it would appear. Home-made lemon curd is gorgeous, but I purposely haven't included a recipe as that would certainly not count as low-faff. There are some really good jars of lemon curd available, and I would urge you to splash out on a really fine one, rather than the scary luminous stuff that you have to cut your way through. The crème fraîche is optional, but I think the combination is just delicious. This recipe is used throughout the book where lemon cupcakes are called for – just leave out the lemon curd and crème fraîche.

✴ Makes about 12

110 g/4 oz/1 cup self-raising flour
110 g/4 oz/½ cup caster
   (superfine) sugar
110 g/4 oz/½ cup margarine,
   softened
1 tsp baking powder
2 large free-range eggs
grated zest of 2 large unwaxed
   lemons, plus extra shreds, to
   decorate (optional)
1 tbsp freshly squeezed lemon
   juice
1 x 350 g/12 oz jar lemon curd
200 ml/7 fl oz crème fraîche

Preheat the oven to 170°C/325°F/Gas mark 3. Line a 12-hole muffin tin (pan) with cupcake cases (baking cups).

Sift the flour and sugar into a large bowl, food processor or mixer. Add all the other ingredients except the lemon curd and crème fraîche, and beat until light and fluffy.

Place heaped teaspoonsful of the mixture (batter) in the prepared cases, and bake in the oven for about 20 minutes until firm to the touch and golden. Remove from the oven and allow to cool.

Once cool, use a small, sharp knife to slice the top off each cake, place a generous spoonful of lemon curd on top of the cake and put the lid back on.

Top the whole shebang with a dollop of crème fraîche and a few tiny shreds of lemon zest if you wish.

Coffee and walnut cupcakes

Another classic. These are firm favourites, even though they are distinctly lacking in gaudiness. I love the old-fashionedness of them – that and the fact that they are absolutely delicious.

✳ Makes about 12

110 g/4 oz/1 cup self-raising flour
110 g/4 oz/½ cup caster (superfine) sugar
110 g/4 oz/½ cup margarine, softened
1 tsp baking powder
2 large free-range eggs
3 tbsp instant coffee granules diluted in 1½ tbsp boiling water
50 g/2 oz/scant ½ cup chopped walnuts, plus 12 walnut halves for decoration

For the icing
200 g/7 oz/⅓ cup icing (confectioners') sugar, sifted
2 tbsp instant coffee granules diluted in 2 tbsp boiling water

Preheat the oven to 170°C/325°F/Gas mark 3. Line a 12-hole muffin tin (pan) with cupcake cases (baking cups).

Sift the flour and sugar into a large bowl, food processor or mixer. Add the margarine, baking powder and eggs, and beat really well until pale and fluffy. Add 1 tablespoon of the coffee mixture. This may be enough – don't add the rest if you don't need to. You don't want the mixture (batter) to be too liquid. Fold in the chopped walnuts, and spoon the mixture into the prepared cases. Bake in the oven for about 20 minutes until firm to the touch. Remove from the oven and allow to cool.

To make the icing, put the icing sugar in a bowl. Add the very strong coffee bit by bit. If the mixture is too stiff, add a few more drops of boiling water. If the coffee flavour is too strong for you, do dilute the mixture to your taste. Spoon the icing over the cooled cupcakes, and dot the top of each one with a walnut half.

Black Forest
gateau cupcakes

Now, I am not ashamed to say that I have a huge fondness for kitsch.
I love things such as avocado and prawns, scampi in a basket and small
things lined up on cocktail sticks or toothpicks. So it really should come
as no surprise that Black Forest gateau should make an appearance.
These things might not be fashionable, but, by George, they taste good.

✱ Makes about 12

85 g/3 oz/¾ cup self-raising
   flour
4 tbsp cocoa powder
110 g/4 oz/½ cup caster
   (superfine) sugar
110 g/4 oz/½ cup margarine,
   softened
1 tsp baking powder
2 large free-range eggs
1 x 450 g/1 lb jar black cherry
   jam
200 ml/7 fl oz double (whipping)
   cream, whipped
60 g/2 oz dark (bittersweet)
   chocolate (at least 70% cocoa
   solids), grated
glacé cherries, to decorate
   (optional)

Preheat the oven to 170°C/325°F/Gas mark 3. Line a
12-hole muffin tin (pan) with cupcake cases (baking cups).

Sift the flour, cocoa powder and sugar into a large bowl, food
processor or mixer. Add the margarine, baking powder and
eggs. Beat well until the mixture (batter) is light and fluffy.
Spoon the mixture into the prepared cases, and bake in the
oven for about 20 minutes until firm to the touch.

Remove from the oven and allow to cool.

Once cool, smother the top of each cupcake with a generous
amount of the jam – you could also use a jar of cherries
that have been soaked in kirsch, yum, yum – then pile
the whipped cream on top. Finish with some grated dark
chocolate. And a cherry on a cocktail stick (toothpick),
if you dare.

Chocolate Maltesers cupcakes

How can anyone not love this? So easy.

Makes about 12

85 g/3 oz/¾ cup self-raising flour
4 tbsp cocoa powder
110 g/4 oz/½ cup caster (superfine) sugar
110 g/4 oz/½ cup margarine, softened
2 large free-range eggs
1 tsp baking powder
2 tsp milk
1 x 400 g/13 oz jar of Nutella or other chocolate hazelnut spread
bag of Maltesers or other chocolate malted milk balls (size depends on your generosity)

Preheat the oven to 170°C/325°F/Gas mark 3. Line a 12-hole muffin tin (pan) with cupcake cases (baking cups).

Sift the flour, cocoa powder and sugar into a large bowl, food processor or mixer. Plonk in all the cake ingredients and whisk away until pale and fluffy (use an electric whisk if you are using a large bowl). Plop heaped teaspoons of the mixture (batter) into the prepared cases, and bake in the oven for around 20 minutes until firm and springy to the touch. Remove from the oven and allow to cool.

Once cool, spread Nutella on top of each cupcake, then place Maltesers on top. You can be as generous as you want. If you want to create a veritable tower (and why wouldn't you – unless you've eaten them all already?), use a splodge of Nutella to glue the Maltesers together.

Banana cupcakes with cream cheese frosting

Banana cake is another classic yummy treat that translates really well to a cupcake. I find that this cake is usually very sweet, so I like to add a little zing with lime zest and, rather than make a sugary icing, top them with a cream cheese frosting, which also adds a little sharpness. The frosting here does contain sugar, but, if you wish, you could easily make the frosting from the Carrot Cupcakes recipe (p.30) and add lime zest instead of orange.

✳ Makes about 12–15, depending on size of bananas

250 g/9 oz/1 cup plus 2 tbsp butter
225 g/8 oz/1 cup caster (superfine) sugar
2 large free-range eggs
3 large ripe bananas, mashed
375 g/13 oz/3¼ cups self-raising flour
75 ml/2½ fl oz milk
grated zest of 1 lime
1 tsp lime juice
dried banana chips (optional), to decorate

For the cream cheese frosting
250 g/9 oz/4 cups icing (confectioners') sugar
125 g/4½ oz/generous ½ cup cream cheese
grated zest and juice of 1 lime

Preheat the oven to 180°C/350°F/Gas mark 4. Line a 12-hole muffin tin (pan) with cupcake cases (baking cups).

Whisk the butter and sugar together until really pale and fluffy. Add the eggs and continue to whisk. The mixture will curdle at this stage – I've never known it not to. Don't worry about it. Add the bananas and then sift the flour on top, and fold it in. Add the milk and lime zest and juice, and fold again until everything is incorporated.

Bake in the oven for 20–25 minutes until firm on top and golden brown.

While the cupcakes are in the oven, make the frosting. Sift the icing sugar over the cream cheese and beat well. Add the zest and the juice, if needed, but don't let the frosting get too runny.

Once the cupcakes have cooled, smother them with the frosting and top with a dried banana chip, if using.

Ginger and lemon cupcakes

This is from the "grown-up" fold, but children do like them! It's just that there is a distinct absence of glitter and colouring, and a general lack of over-the-topness. How peculiar.

* Makes about 12

110 g/4 oz/1 cup self-raising flour
110 g /4 oz/½ cup caster
  (superfine) sugar
110 g/4 oz/½ cup margarine,
  softened
1 tsp baking powder
1 tsp ground ginger
grated zest and juice of
  1 unwaxed lemon
2 large free-range eggs
50 g/2 oz crystallized (candied)
  ginger, chopped, plus extra,
  to decorate
200 g/7 oz/1⅓ cups icing sugar,
  sifted

Preheat the oven to 170°C/325°F/Gas mark 3. Line a 12-hole muffin tin (pan) with cupcake cases (baking cups).

Sift the flour and sugar into a mixing bowl, food processor or mixer. Add the margarine, baking powder, ground ginger, lemon zest and eggs. Beat well until light and fluffy. Fold in the chopped crystallized ginger. Spoon the mixture (batter) into the prepared cases, and bake in the oven for about 20 minutes until golden and firm to the touch. Remove from the oven and allow to cool.

Make the icing by slowly adding the lemon juice to the icing sugar and mixing well. If you need a little more liquid, add a few drops of boiling water. You are looking for the consistency of thick soup.

When the cakes are cool, spoon the icing over and top with a little chunk of the extra ginger.

Easy-peasy heart cupcakes

Yes, there is some piping here. No, it isn't tricky. Royal icing is invaluable for piping. You can use it for icing cakes if you like a very hard surface. What I suggest you do if you are a bit nervous about your piping skills is to practise on a plate or directly onto your work surface. When you are happy that you have the flow of the shape right, go for it! Let the base layer of icing dry really well before you start piping. If you want to pipe something other than hearts, do it. Tiny spots all over look really pretty and couldn't be simpler.

✳ Makes around 12

1 quantity of basic cupcakes (see p.18)
1 quantity of glacé icing (see p.17)
2 tbsp royal icing (see p.17)
food colourings (preferably gel)

✳ *You will need a parchment piping (decorating) bag*

Make the cupcakes as for the recipe on p.24, and allow them to cool.

To make the glacé icing, sift the icing sugar into a bowl, and add the water drop by drop until you get the consistency you require (thick soup). Add the food colouring, and check that you still have the correct consistency – you may need to add a little more sifted icing sugar. Spoon the icing over the cakes and leave to dry. Leaving them for a couple of hours at this stage is really good, if you can.

Tint the royal icing with the food colouring, then use some to fill the parchment piping (decorating) bag, squeezing the icing down to the end.

Snip the very end off the bag. Practise piping the hearts or whatever shape you want, then pipe away to your heart's content on the top of each iced cupcake (geddit?). Leave to dry for another hour or two before scoffing.

Grown-up mocha cupcakes

The coffee in the buttercream makes these a bit more adult, and the sponge has that slight hint of bitterness that is needed to cut through all that topping. I think that you will find that most very grown-up and sensible people who wouldn't usually think about eating a cupcake will be like putty in your hands if you offer them these.

✳ Makes about 12

85 g/3 oz/³/4 cup self-raising flour
4 tbsp cocoa powder
110 g/4 oz/½ cup caster (superfine) sugar
110 g/4 oz/½ cup margarine, softened
1 tsp baking powder
2 tbsp instant coffee granules dissolved in 2 tsp boiling water
2 large free-range eggs
25 g/1 oz chocolate coffee beans (optional)
gold dragees (optional), to decorate

For the mocha buttercream
110 g/4 oz/½ cup unsalted butter, softened
225 g/8 oz/1½ cups icing (confectioners') sugar
1 tbsp cocoa powder
1 tbsp instant coffee dissolved in 2 tsp boiling water

✳ *You will need a large piping (decorating) bag fitted with a star nozzle (tube)*

Preheat the oven to 170°C/325°F/Gas mark 3. Line a 12-hole muffin tin (pan) with cupcake cases (baking cups).

Sift the flour, cocoa and sugar into a mixing bowl, food processor or mixer. Add the margarine, baking powder, dissolved coffee and eggs, and beat well until the mixture (batter) is light and fluffy. (If you want to add a real bonus feature, chuck in a small handful of chocolate coffee beans and fold them in.) Spoon the mixture into the prepared cases, and bake in the oven for around 20 minutes until firm to the touch. Remove from the oven and allow to cool.

To make the buttercream, put the butter in a bowl. Sift the icing sugar and cocoa over the top, and beat away. Add the coffee and beat again. If the mixture is too wet, add a bit more sifted icing sugar. Bit dry? Add a tiny bit more coffee.

Place a piping (decorating) bag with a star nozzle into a beaker, and fill the bag with the icing. Pipe huge, glamorous swirls onto the cakes, and dot with gold dragees, if you so wish.

Extremely posh but nevertheless low-faff rose cupcakes

Now, these aren't cheap, but, heavens to Betsy, they look good, don't they? I make quite a lot of these, and I do still feel slightly embarrassed when people go all gooey over them. I mean, they can't realize that this is the ultimate in "plonking" cakes. Again, I say to you: sssssshhhhh. These cakes could also be made in lemon by following the recipe for the lemon cupcakes on p.32 and omitting the lemon curd, and also making up the icing with lemon juice, rather than water.

✳ Makes about 12

1 quantity of basic cupcakes
   (see p.18)
200 g/7 oz/1⅓ cups icing sugar,
   sifted
boiling water
gel food colouring
12 sugar (candied) roses

✳ TOP TIP:

These sugar roses are made from flower paste (essentially a sugar paste that dries very hard) and can be bought from sugarcraft shops. They are readily available from on-line sugarcraft shops in a variety of colours and sizes.

Make the cupcakes as for the recipe on p.24, and allow them to cool.

To make the icing, put the icing sugar in a bowl, and slowly add boiling water until you have a thick soup consistency. Add the food colouring and pour over cakes. Wait about 10 minutes before carefully placing (plonking) a rose on top of each cupcake.

Voilà.

Cupcakes with mascarpone and fruit

This recipe works really well as a dessert after a lovely summery lunch.
You can make it with either vanilla or lemon cupcakes – both delicious.
This is another of those recipes that can look staggeringly beautiful,
but is criminally easy.

✳ Makes about 12

1 quantity of basic cupcakes
   (see p.24) or lemon cupcakes
   (see p.32)
250 g/9 oz mascarpone cheese
selection of soft ripe fruit such
   as blueberries, strawberries,
   raspberries, peaches
   and nectarines

Make the cupcakes as for the recipe on p.24 or p.32, and
allow them to cool.

Empty the tub of mascarpone cheese into a bowl and give it
a bit of a beating, but don't add anything to it. Place a dollop
of mascarpone on top of each of the cupcakes, and artfully
arrange the fruit on and around the cakes.

✳ VARIATION:
If you are using lemon cakes,
add a little lemon curd to the
mascarpone, top the cakes
with this, then spoon over
passion fruit pulp.

Cupcakes à la Battenburg

I love the colour combination of Battenburg and toyed with the idea of wrapping the whole caboodle in marzipan, but I settled on this version. I like the tang of the apricot jam, but you could use any other flavour. You don't have to stick to pink sponge, either. Why not green and blue?

✳ Makes about 24

220 g/8 oz/2 cups self-raising flour
220 g/8 oz/1 cup caster (superfine) sugar
220 g/8 oz/1 cup margarine, softened
2 tsp baking powder
4 large free-range eggs
2 tsp pure vanilla extract
pink food colouring (preferably gel)
apricot jam for spreading
1 quantity lemon glacé icing (p.17)
dolly mixture or other sprinkles, to decorate

Preheat oven to 160°C/325°F/Gas mark 3. Grease two 20cm/8 in square cake tins (pans), and line with baking parchment.

Sift the flour and sugar into a mixing bowl, food processor or food mixer. Add the margarine, baking powder, eggs and vanilla. Beat until light and fluffy. Divide the mixture (batter) into two equal portions in separate bowls, and add a little bit of pink food colouring to one half. Pour each cake mixture into a separate tin, and bake in the oven for 20–25 minutes until firm to the touch and golden. Don't worry that the pink cake doesn't look very pink. Remove from the oven and turn both cakes onto wire racks to cool.

Using a sharp knife, level the tops of the cakes so that the top and the bottom are completely flat. Spread a thin layer of apricot jam over the upper side of the pink layer. Place the plain cake on top so that the bottom side of the sponge faces upwards. Cut into 2 cm/¾ in strips.

Now, pay attention. Lay one strip on its side so that you have a line of pink and a line of yellow. Spread a thin layer of jam over the top. Take another strip of cake and lay it on its side on top of the jammy strip, but reversed so that pale lies directly on top of pink and vice versa. Cut these strips into squares, and drizzle with the glacé icing. Let some of the icing dribble down the sides. Plop a dolly mixture (or alternative adornment) on top, and place in cupcake cases.

Bite my cherry

Yes, yes, this is my version of the cherry Bakewell tart, one of my all-time favourite cakes. But, get this – no fat, no flour and contains fruit and nuts. Not only is it perfectly wonderful for gluten-intolerant person-ages, but also it must somehow count as "good for you". Surely?

❊ Makes about 12

4 large free-range eggs, separated
175 g/6 oz/¾ cup caster
    (superfine) sugar
225 g/8 oz/2¼ cups ground
    almonds
1 tsp baking powder (or ½ tsp
    bicarbonate of soda (baking
    soda) and 1 tsp cream of
    tartar if you want to keep it
    gluten-free)
12 glacé (candied) cherries

For the decoration
1 quantity lemon glacé icing
    (p.17)
golf ball-sized piece of sugar
    paste (rolled fondant)
red food colouring (preferably gel)
edible glue
red edible glitter
green food colouring
    (preferably gel)
1 tbsp royal icing (see p.17)

❊ *You will need a parchment
    piping (decorating) bag*

Preheat the oven to 200°C/400°F/Gas mark 6. Line a 12-hole muffin tin (pan) with cupcake cases (baking cups).

Beat the egg yolks and sugar together until pale. In a clean, dry separate bowl, whisk the egg whites until stiff peaks form. Gently fold them into the egg yolk mixture, then fold in the ground almonds and baking powder. Spoon the mixture (batter) into the prepared cases, and push 1 cherry down into each sponge. Bake in the oven for 15–20 minutes, keeping an eye on them throughout – burnt almond doesn't taste good. Remove from the oven and allow to cool.

Make a glacé icing (p.17) and pour a little over each cake. While you are waiting for the icing to set (30 minutes), make the sugar paste cherries. Dye the sugar paste red by dipping a cocktail stick (toothpick) into the red food colouring and transferring it to the paste. Knead the colour in evenly, then make little cherry-sized balls (one for each cupcake), paint them with the edible glue and roll them in the edible glitter.

When the icing is dry, add a little food colouring to the royal icing to make it green. Fill a parchment piping (decorating) bag with the royal icing, squeezing the icing down to the end. Snip the very end off the bag. Stick a sugar paste cherry onto each cupcake with a tiny blob of edible glue, and pipe green stalks and leaves with the green royal icing.

A lemony little-bitta-glitta

Discovering edible glitter was a high point in my cake decorating life. It really is fantastic stuff. And what's more, what goes in, must come out, as glitter is poorly absorbed by the body ... need I go on? Of course, you needn't stick to hearts. Go with whatever shape takes your fancy. Go mad with colour and glitter. It's what it's there for.

* Makes about 12

1 quantity of lemon cupcakes
   (see Lemonylicious, p.32)
cornflour (cornstarch)
   for dusting
sugar paste (rolled fondant)
edible glue
edible glitter
food colouring (preferably gel)
1 quantity lemon glacé icing
   (p.17)

* *You will need a heart-shaped
pastry cutter and a small
clean paintbrush*

Make the cupcakes as the recipe on p. 32, and allow to cool.

Dust a work surface or clean board with cornflour (cornstarch) and knead a piece of sugar paste (rolled fondant) the size of a golf ball until it softens and becomes pliable. Dust a rolling pin with some more cornflour, and roll out the sugar paste until it is about 3 mm/⅛in thick.

Cut out 12 hearts (or as many cakes as you have) using a heart-shaped pastry cutter, and brush them lightly with edible glue. Tip a pile of glitter onto a plate, and carefully lower the hearts glue-side down onto the glitter. Carefully lift off so that you have a completely glitter-covered heart. Place onto another cornflour-dusted plate, right-side up, and continue with the others.

Make the glacé icing (see p.17) and tint whatever colour you choose, and spoon the icing over the cakes. Let both the icing and the glitter hearts dry out. The hearts are much easier to handle if they've been given a bit of air.

Put a tiny blob of edible glue on the centre of each cake, and carefully place (no plonking, please) a heart on top. Beautiful.

Lemony lustres

Now, with this cake I have used the traditional way of making a Victoria sponge, which is why I have included it in the mid-faff section. It's not tricky – just slower than the bung-it-all-in method I love so much. Edible lustre comes as a powder in tiny tubes from sugarcraft shops.

✱ Makes about 12

110 g/4 oz/½ cup butter, softened
110 g/4 oz/½ cup caster (superfine) sugar
2 large free-range eggs, beaten
110 g/4 oz/1 cup self-raising flour, sifted
1 tsp baking powder
grated zest of 1 unwaxed lemon
1 tbsp freshly squeezed lemon juice

For the decoration
1 quantity glacé icing (p.17)
gel food colouring (optional)
1 tbsp royal icing (see p.17)
edible lustre (available from cake decorating and sugarcraft shops)
½ tsp vodka or other clear alcohol

✱ *You will need a small paintbrush*

Preheat the oven to 170°C/325°F/Gas mark 3. Line a 12-hole muffin tin (pan) with cupcake cases (baking cups).

Cream the butter and sugar together until really pale and fluffy. Slowly add the beaten eggs, beating well after each addition. Sift the flour and baking powder onto the mixture (batter) and, using a large metal spoon, carefully fold it in. Add the lemon zest and, if the mixture looks a little stiff, add the juice a little at a time (it may not be necessary). Fold again. The mixture should gently plop off the spoon. Spoon into the prepared cases, and bake in the oven for 20–25 minutes until golden and firm to the touch. Remove from the oven and allow to cool.

Make the glacé icing (see p.17) and colour as required. Spoon over the cooled cakes. When the icing has dried, put the royal icing into a piping (decorating) bag with a fine nozzle (tube), and pipe a large heart onto each cupcake. Wait for this to harden slightly – around an hour.

To finish, tip ½ teaspoon of the lustre onto a saucer or into a small bowl. Add some vodka to the lustre drop by drop. Mix with the paintbrush until you have a consistency just a tiny bit looser than a paste. Leave the alcohol to evaporate – the mixture will thicken up slightly. Carefully brush the lustre mixture over the piped heart and let it dry.

Choc-a-doodle-do

This is my version of a chocolate brownie. It is not, however, as heavy as a brownie. There's something unappealing about picking up a cupcake and being able to use it as a doorstop. It's wrong. So I've just taken the key elements of the brownie: chocolate, nuts, chocolate and chocolate.

* Makes about 12

4 large free-range eggs, separated
150 g/5 oz/1⅔ cups caster (superfine) sugar
3 tsp cocoa powder
225 g/8 oz/2¼ cups ground almonds
1 tsp baking powder
50 g/1¾ oz/scant ½ cup chopped mixed nuts (such as hazlenuts, walnuts, almonds)
small bag of Maltesers or other chocolate malted milk balls

For the chocolate ganache
2 x 100 g/3½ oz bars of good-quality dark (bittersweet) chocolate (at least 70% cocoa solids)
200 ml/7 fl oz double (whipping) cream

Preheat the oven to 200°C/400°F/Gas mark 6. Line a 12-hole muffin tin (pan) with cupcake cases (baking cups).

Whisk the eggs and sugar together until pale and creamy. In a clean separate bowl, whisk the egg whites until stiff peaks form, then gently fold into the egg yolk mixture. Sift over the cocoa and fold in with the almonds, baking powder and chopped nuts. Lightly bash half the packet of Maltesers – you want large chunks, rather than powder – and fold these into the mixture. Spoon the mixture into the prepared cases, and bake in the oven for 15–20 minutes.

Make the ganache by putting the chocolate, still in its wrapper, onto a hard surface. Grab a rolling pin and smash the living daylights out of that chocolate. Open it all up carefully over a bowl and, hey presto! Gravel chocolate. Just make sure none of the wrapper goes in with the choc.

Heat the cream in a small heavy saucepan until almost boiling, then pour over the chocolate. Leave for 30 seconds before gently stirring it all together. Carefully spoon the ganache on top of the cupcakes, and top each one with a leftover Malteser if you haven't eaten them all. There probably won't be enough for all the cakes, so you might as well eat them ...

No-nonsense chocolate on chocolate

When I want a cupcake, this tends to be one I go for. It hits all the right spots. Moist, dark chocolatey sponge and a thick layer of almost fudge-like dark chocolate ganache on top. Stand with your eyes closed as you savour every last morsel. Feel those endorphins releasing themselves.

Makes about 12, but you may choose to say that there were only 6

60 g/2 oz/½ cup self-raising flour
60 g/2 oz/½ cup good-quality unsweetened cocoa powder
1 tsp baking powder
110 g/4 oz/½ cup caster (superfine) sugar
110 g/4 oz/½ cup margarine, softened
2 large free-range eggs
2 tbsp milk
150 g/5 oz good-quality dark (bittersweet) chocolate (at least 70% cocoa solids)
100 g/3½ oz good-quality milk chocolate
200 ml/7 fl oz double (whipping) cream

Preheat the oven to 160°C/325°F/Gas mark 3. Line a 12-hole muffin tin (pan) with cupcake cases (baking cups).

Sift the flour, cocoa, baking powder and sugar into a large bowl, food processor or mixer. Add the margarine and eggs, and beat away until light and fluffy. I think it's worthwhile to stop the mixer after a few moments and scrape everything down the sides of the bowl, so that you know none of the cocoa gets stuck. Beat again. If the mixture looks quite stiff, add enough of the milk and beat, so that you get the mixture (batter) plopping nicely off a spoon. Spoon into the prepared cases, and bake for 20 minutes, or until firm on top. Let the cakes cool and get on with the ganache.

Bash all the chocolate to smithereens as in Choc-a-doodle-do (opposite). (If the chocolate is not still in its packet, do this between two pieces of greaseproof or waxed paper.) Tip into a bowl. Put the cream in a small heavy saucepan and bring it to the boiling point, then pour over the chocolate. Leave for 30 seconds before gently stirring it all together. (This ganache differs slightly in that I've fiddled with the ratio of chocolate to cream, and added a smidgen of milk chocolate.) Spoon the ganache over the top of the cupcakes. Embellish as you wish.

Chocolate "fondant" cupcakes

OK, I've cheated. So, for legal reasons, I've put the word "fondant" in quotation marks. When I say "fondant", what I actually mean is "Well, there's a gooey, chocolatey centre that is a bit like a fondant. But look, I'm trying to give you a delicious cake, OK? So don't go getting all cross and literal on me." Will that do?

✳ Makes 12

110 g/4 oz/½ cup soft margarine
85 g/3 oz/generous ½ cup self-
    raising (self-rising) flour, sifted
25 g/1 oz/¼ cup cocoa powder
    (unsweetened cocoa)
110 g/4 oz/½ cup caster
    (superfine) sugar
2 large eggs
1 tsp vanilla extract
12 heaped teaspoons of Nutella
    (or other chocolate spread)
icing (confectioners') sugar, for
    dusting

Preheat the oven to 180°C/350°F/Gas Mark 4. Line a 12-hole muffin tin (pan) with cases.

In a large bowl, or preferably a mixer, put in all the ingredients apart from the Nutella. Whisk for 5 minutes, or until you have a light, almost moussey texture.

Divide the mixture between the 12 cupcake cases – don't worry about smoothing the surfaces, just plop it in. Bake for 15–20 minutes, or until firm on top, and risen and slightly springy to the touch.

Leave the cupcakes in the muffin tin for 2 minutes, then take a small sharp knife and cut out a conical shape from the top of each cupcake. Pop 1 heaped teaspoon of Nutella into each hole and put the lid back on. Press down gently, then sprinkle a tiny bit of icing (confectioners') sugar over the top of each cake.

Serve while just warm, when the Nutella is still liquid and oozy. However, eating them cold is not a disaster, just texturally different.

Love letters

Cupcakes were invented for declarations of love, surely? Valentine's Day is a particularly busy time for me, and the "I love you" box has become a bit of a classic. Although it looks lovely in oranges and reds, I also did a really nice one for a bloke in greens and purples.

✳ Makes about 12

1 quantity of basic cupcakes in
    vanilla or lemon (p.24)
1 quantity glacé icing (p.17)
red, orange and ruby food
    colouring (preferably gel)
golf ball-sized piece of sugar
    paste (rolled fondant)
cornflour (cornstarch)
1 tbsp royal icing (p.17)
edible glue

✳ *You will need a piping*
   (decorating) bag with a fine
   writing nozzle (tube) and
   1 small and 1 tiny heart-
   shaped cutter

Have your cupcakes ready. Make the glacé icing (p.17) and divide the mixture among three bowls. Colour each bowl with orange, ruby and red food colouring, using one colour for each bowl. Divide the sugar paste into three, and also colour these to the same intensity in their respective colours as the icing, kneading the colour in evenly. Lightly dust a work surface with cornflour (cornstarch) and roll out each of the sugar pastes until about 3 mm/⅛ in thick. Cut 4 small and 4 tiny hearts out of each colour. Leave to dry on a cornflour-dusted plate for at least 1 hour.

Ice the cupcakes so that you have four each of each colour, and leave to dry. With the orange cakes, stick a large ruby heart in the middle with a small red heart on top. With the ruby cakes, stick on a large red heart with an orange tiny one. With the red cakes, stick a large orange heart with a small ruby heart. Leave overnight to dry.

Fill a piping (decorating) bag with a fine nozzle (tube) with the royal icing. Squeeze the icing right to the end. Line the cupcakes up in three rows of four, keeping the same colour in each row, so you can keep an eye on what is piped where. Pipe "I" across one cupcake, "love" across another and "you" across a third. Pipe tiny white dots all around the edge of all of the cakes, and put a central dot on all the cakes that don't have writing on. A large piped kiss wouldn't go amiss.

Cupid's cupcakes

I have one word to say here: "silicone" – the most wonderful invention in the world of baking tins (pans). They are just fantastic. You don't need to line them or even grease them. For these cupcakes, you really do need to invest in a silicone heart-shaped muffin tray.

✳ Makes about 8

110 g/4 oz/1 cup self-raising flour
110 g/4 oz/½ cup caster
   (superfine) sugar
1 tsp baking powder
110 g/4 oz/½ cup margarine,
   softened
2 large free-range eggs
1 tsp pure vanilla extract
1 quantity lemon or plain glacé
   icing (p.17)
food colouring (preferably gel)
1 tbsp royal icing (see p.17)
edible lustre
vodka

✳ *You will need a silicone heart-shaped muffin tray, metallic foil .a piping (decorating) bag with a fine size 2 nozzle (tube)*

✳ *Pictured here with the Floribunda Cupcacus recipe, see p.64.*

Preheat the oven to 170°C/325°F/Gas mark 3.

Sift the flour, sugar and baking powder into a bowl, food processor or mixer. Add the margarine, eggs and vanilla, and beat until pale and fluffy. Spoon the mixture (batter) carefully into the silicone muffin tray, place on a metal baking sheet and bake in the oven for about 20 minutes, until golden and firm to the touch. Let the cupcakes cool in the muffin tray, then turn them out onto a wire rack.

Slice the tops off the cupcakes so that you have a level surface and turn the cakes upside down. You want to ice the bottoms of the cakes. Make the glacé icing (p.17) and tint whatever colour your heart desires (sorry). Drizzle the icing all over the cakes and let it run down the sides.

Before the icing is completely dry, lay out all your metallic cupcake cases (baking cups). Dip your fingers into a bowl of cold water, then lift the cakes onto the cases – this stops the icing sticking to your fingers. Carefully mould the cases around the hearts, and the cases should stay put.

When the icing is completely dry, pipe decorations onto the cakes in royal icing. Let that dry. Mix some edible lustre with a few drops of vodka (see Lemony Lustres, p.51), and paint onto the royal icing. Alternatively, you could paint the entire top with edible glue and dip into glitter. Wooo-hooo!

Boys' own

I like the idea of a masculine cupcake! Well, if there are cupcakes with frocks and shoes, it's only fair that the chaps should have something. Let us not forget that men are huge consumers of cake, although they may pretend they aren't that bothered. Right. The idea for these came while my son was watching the original Batman. High art indeed.

✳ Makes about 12

1 quantity of lemon or basic
   vanilla cupcakes (see p.24 or
   p.32)
1 quantity glacé icing (p.17)
gel food colouring in assorted
   colours
2 tbsp royal icing (see p.17)

✳ *You will need 3 piping
(decorating) bags fitted with
fine nozzles (tubes)*

Make the cupcakes according to whichever recipe you choose, and leave to cool.

Make the glacé icing with the icing (confectioners') sugar and either the lemon juice or water. Colour the icing a really deep blue or green or brown. Cover the cakes with the icing and let them dry really well. With colour this dark, it is important that the icing is as dry as possible before you start piping.

Divide the royal icing into three bowls, and tint them whatever colour the chap likes. The royal icing needs to be really firm, so if it's a bit on the loose side add a little more sifted icing sugar. Pipe on appropriately butch comic-strip-type words, such as "BIFF", "POW" and "ZAP". Word of warning: if you pipe on the words before the icing underneath has dried, or if the royal icing is too wet, the darker colour will bleed into the piping.

A star is born

Stars are great on cupcakes. First, they look fantastic; secondly, everyone loves them; and, thirdly, they are dead easy. Marvellous. Mixing up styles of stars onto a plateful of cupcakes looks great.

☀ Makes about 12

1 quantity of basic vanilla or lemon cupcakes (see p.24 or p.32)
1 quantity glacé icing (p.17)
gel food colouring
golf ball-sized piece of sugar paste (rolled fondant)
cornflour (cornstarch) for dusting
2 tbsp royal icing (see p.17)
edible glue
silver dragees

☀ *You will need 3 piping (decorating) bags with fine nozzles (tubes), a star-shaped cutter and a clean paintbrush*

Make up the cupcakes and leave to cool. Make up the glacé icing (p.16) and divide the icing into two bowls. Leave one batch of icing white, and gently tint the other a pale blue. Ice the cakes so that half the cakes have white icing on them, while the remaining cakes are iced in blue. Leave to dry.

Tint the sugar paste (rolled fondant) with gel to an intense blue. Knead the colour in evenly. Dust a work surface with a little cornflour (cornflour), and roll out the sugar paste to about 3 mm/⅛ in thick. Cut out 6 stars.

Divide the royal icing into three bowls and tint each bowl with the food colouring – you can use the same colour, i.e. blue, in different intensities, so that you end up with three distinctly different tones of blue. Put the icing into three separate piping (decorating) bags with fine nozzles (tubes), pushing the icing down to the end of each bag.

Place a blob of edible glue on three of the white cakes and three of the blue cakes, and stick a star to each. Take the palest royal icing and pipe a blob into the middle of the star. Place a dragee on top of the blob.

For the other cakes, pipe a 5-pointed star with whatever colour you like. Pipe five dots between the outer points of the star in another colour. Using the most intense colour, pipe a small circle in the centre of the star. Fill in the circle with contrasting icing, then finally add a tiny blob of the third colour to the top.

Floribunda cupcacus

These roses can look very pretty, or completely over the top and vulgar. It really depends on the size, colour and the free hand with the glitter that transforms the flower from tasteful to trashy. I know which I prefer ...

Makes about 12

golf ball-sized piece of sugar paste (rolled fondant)
gel food colouring in assorted colours
cornflour (cornstarch) for dusting
edible glitter (optional)
1 quantity of lemon or basic vanilla cupcakes (see p.32 or p.24)
1 quantity of fondant icing (see p.19)
edible glue

You will find these pictured on p.59.

Make the roses first, the day before if possible. Separate the sugar paste (rolled fondant) into as many portions as you want colours and tint with the food colouring. Knead the colour in evenly. Lightly dust a work surface with cornflour (cornstarch). Take a marble-sized piece of sugar paste and divide it in two. Take one piece and roll it into a small fat sausage. On the work surface, flatten in slightly and try to keep one long edge a bit thinner than the other longer edge. Repeat with the other piece. Start rolling one sausage up, with the thinner layer being the "top" of the rose. Just before you finish rolling, insert the second flattened sausage under the flap of the first one and keep rolling. Voila! You should have a rose type flower. You'll probably find that it is a bit cylindrical with a lumpy bottom. Leave the rose sitting up on its lumpy bottom for an hour or two, then slice the bottom off with a sharp knife. Continue making roses until you go mad.

If you want a glittery rose, tip some edible glitter onto a saucer and lightly dip the top of the rose in the glitter – you shouldn't need any glue. Leave to dry for at least 4 hours.

Make the cupcakes in whichever recipe you choose. Allow to cool, then cover with fondant icing, tinted with a colour of your choice. Let the icing dry completely. Carefully stick a small blob of edible glue under each rose, and place on the cupcakes, either individually or in a mixed posy.

Mid-faff insects

I say "mid-faff" because there are also "high-faff" insects. I don't think I have an unhealthy preoccupation; it's just that insects lend themselves to cupcake embellishment extremely well.

✳ Makes about 12

1 quantity of lemon or basic vanilla cupcakes (see p.32 or p.24)
1 quantity glacé icing (p.17)
golf ball-sized piece of sugar paste (rolled fondant)
gel food colouring
cornflour (cornstarch) for dusting
edible glue
1 tbsp royal icing (see p.17)
coloured dragees (optional)

✳ *You will need butterfly cutters and 2 or 3 piping (decorating) bags with fine nozzles (tubes) (depending on how many colours you want to use)*

Make the cupcakes according to whichever recipe you choose, and leave to cool. Make the glacé icing (p.17) and colour as you wish. Ice the cakes and leave to dry.

To make the butterflies, tint some of the sugar paste (rolled fondant) with the food colouring. Knead the colour in evenly. Lightly dust a work surface with cornflour (cornstarch) and roll out the paste until it is about 3 mm/⅛ in thick. Cut out the butterflies and leave to dry for 30 minutes or so.

Meanwhile, you can get on with the ladybirds. Tint some sugar paste red, and another very small amount black. Knead both balls separately until the colour is even. Depending on how big you want the ladybirds to be, roll a ball of red paste into a body-type shape. Take a tiny bit of black, and flatten it to make a face. Stick it on one end. Make two tiny sausages of black to make the wing edges. Then make some really tiny balls for the spots. How many spots you manage will depend on how fine your handiwork. Two seems to be my limit ... Poke a little face into the black with the end of a cocktail stick (toothpick), and make some tiny white antenna with white sugar paste.

Everything can be stuck on with edible glue. When the little chap is finished, stick him on the cake and use a little royal icing in a piping (decorating) bag with a fine nozzle (tube) to

(continued on p.66)

(continued from p.65)
surround him with a few piped flowers for company.

Back to the butterflies, stick them onto the cakes with some edible glue. Tint several little batches of royal icing and, using decorating bags fitted with fine nozzles, you can then pipe patterns on the butterfly's wings. Add dragees if you wish. I think these cakes look great with spots piped round the edge of the cake and a dragee popped on the top of each spot.

Butterflies go disco

I have developed a growing stash of cutters. The glitter butterfly remains a firm favourite.

✳ Makes about 12

1 quantity of basic vanilla or lemon cupcakes (p.24 or p.32)
1 quantity glacé icing (p.17)
food colouring (preferably gel)
cornflour (cornstarch) for dusting
golf ball-sized piece of sugar paste (rolled fondant)
edible glitter
edible glue

✳ *You will need butterfly cutters (large, small or both) and a paintbrush*

Make the cupcakes according to whichever recipe you choose, and leave to cool.

Make up the glacé icing (p.17) and colour as you wish. Pour over the cakes and leave to dry.

Dust a little cornflour onto a work surface, and roll out the sugar paste (rolled fondant) until it is about 3 mm/⅛in thick. Cut out butterflies – allow one large butterfly per cake or two small.

Brush a little edible glue all over the butterflies and dip onto the edible glitter that you have poured onto a plate.

Stick the butterflies to the cakes. If you are using two small ones, it looks lovely if you have them flying off in different directions.

Mysteries from the deep

None of these would stand up to close scrutiny from a marine biologist, but we won't worry about that. Very popular with smallish children, these ones. It's one way to get them to eat fish, I suppose.

✳ Makes about 12

1 quantity of lemon or basic
   vanilla cupcakes (see p.32
   or p.24)
1 quantity glacé icing (p.17)
2 tbsp royal icing (p.17)
gel food colouring in assorted
   colours
silver dragees (optional –
   not suitable for very small
   children)

✳ *You will need three or four
   piping (decorating) bags with
   fine nozzles (tubes)*

Make the cupcakes according to whichever recipe you choose, and leave to cool.

Make the glacé icing (p.17) and colour it using the gel food colouring. I think blue or green really works best for these cakes. Ice the cakes and leave to dry.

Meanwhile, divide the royal icing into three or four small bowls, and tint them whatever colour you like. Put the icing in piping (decorating) bags with fine nozzles (tubes), and practise on a plate if you aren't 100 per cent confident. A starfish is really easy to start with – a five-pointed star, filled in with tiny dots. Add a face with different-coloured icing and you're done. Fishes can be outlined, then scales and face filled in with other colours. An octopus looks great with random tiny dots around the body and edging onto the tentacles.

Don't make the designs all the same – have three or four different fish as well as an octopus or a starfish. No rules, just get piping.

Cut-out classics

Cutting shapes out of coloured sugar paste (rolled fondant) is simplicity itself, and the results look great. This recipe is in this chapter only because of the various stages needed – there really is no skill involved at all. Unless you are colour blind, in which case get someone to help you.

* Makes about 12

1 quantity of any sort of cupcake except for chocolate
1 quantity glacé icing (p.17)
gel food colouring in assorted colours
golf ball-sized piece of sugar paste (rolled fondant)
cornflour (cornstarch) for dusting
1 tbsp royal icing (see p.17)
edible glue

* You will need various cutters, several piping (decorating) bags with fine nozzles (tubes) and a paintbrush

Make the cupcakes according to whichever recipe you choose, and leave to cool.

Make the glacé icing with icing (confectioners') sugar and the lemon juice or boiling water, and divide into as many bowls as you want colours. Tint the icing with the food colouring, then ice the cakes. Leave to dry.

Separate the sugar paste (rolled fondant) into as many colours as you want and tint them. Knead the colour in evenly. Dust a work surface with cornflour (cornstarch), and roll out the sugar paste until it is about 3 mm/⅛ in thick. Cut out whatever shapes you like. I usually do hearts, stars and flowers. Leave to dry for about 30 minutes.

Using edible glue, stick a cut-out shape onto a cake of a different colour. Keep going until all the cakes have a shape.

Tint the royal icing into as many colours as you like and, using a piping (decorating) bag with a fine nozzle (tube), pipe a blob onto the middle of each sugar-paste shape. I think it's nice to have a third colour appear on the cake at this point. You may also like to pipe tiny dots all the way round the edge of the cake.

Incredible invertebrates

May I present high-faff dragonflies and bees.

* Makes about 12

1 quantity of lemon or basic
   vanilla cupcakes (see p.32
   or p.24)
1 quantity of fondant icing (p.19)
gel food colourings
golf ball-sized piece of sugar
   paste (rolled fondant)
edible glue
edible glitter
1 tbsp royal icing (see p.17)
dragees for the bees' eyes

* *You will need a paintbrush,
a cocktail stick (toothpick), a
piping (decorating) bag with
a fine nozzle (tube) and a
steady hand*

* *You will find these pictured
on p.67.*

Make the cupcakes in whichever recipe you choose. Allow to
cool, then cover with fondant icing, tinted in colours of your
choice. Let the icing dry completely.

Make the dragonfly wings first. Tint some of the sugar
paste (rolled fondant) whatever colour you want the wings,
kneading the colour in evenly. Take pea-sized pieces and roll
them into tiny sausages and flatten them slightly. You will
need 2 top wings per dragonfly. You also need 2 slightly
smaller bottom wings (petit pois) made the same way. Cover
the wings in edible glue, and roll them in glitter. Leave to dry
for at least 1 hour.

To make the glittery bumble bee, tint some of the sugar
paste a deep yellow and a small amount black. Knead the
colour in evenly. Take broad (fava) bean-sized pieces of the
yellow paste, and roll into cylinder shapes with rounded
ends. Cover in glue and roll in gold glitter. To make the yellow
bee, do the same, but omit the glitter. Leave to dry. Make tiny
black stripes and glue them over the bees. Make a tiny black
sting and stick it to the bee's bottom. Again leave to dry.

Make some tiny white sugar-paste wings and glue them to
the top of the bee using a tiny dab of edible glue. For the
faces, make two indents with a cocktail stick (toothpick), and
pop in some dragees. Draw a smile with the cocktail stick.

Stick the bees onto the cakes using edible glue, and pipe on
a couple of flowers using royal icing. (continued opposite)

Back to the dragonflies. Stick 2 large top and 2 small bottom wings onto a cake. For the body, tint some royal icing a contrasting colour and pipe a thickish line between the wings, starting at the top of the wings and ending well below the bottom wings. At the top of the wings, pipe an extra blob for the head. Stick 2 dragees on for eyes. Stick the dragonflies onto the cakes using edible glue, then pipe any flowers or dots in royal icing around the cupcakes to finish them off.

Blinking butterflies

These butterflies don't blink. The reason they are called "blinking" is that they can sometimes break. But the time and effort you put in should hopefully reward you with a really pretty snazzy invertebrate.

✴ Makes about 12

a little white vegetable fat (vegetable shortening) such as Trex or Crisco
3 tbsp royal icing (see p.17)
food colouring (preferably gel)
1 quantity of cupcakes of your choice
1 quantity of fondant icing (see p.19) or chocolate ganache (see p.52) if you are using chocolate cakes

✴ *You will need a sheet of clear acetate and 2 parchment piping (decorating) bags with fine nozzles (tubes)*

You need to make the butterflies at least 2 days in advance, preferably even earlier. Draw the outline of the butterfly's wings on a piece of paper, and repeat so that the whole sheet is covered in butterfly wings. Place the acetate over the paper and wipe over a very thin layer of white vegetable fat.

With 2 tbsp of the royal icing, tinted whatever colour you want the wings to be, fill a piping (decorating) bag with a fine nozzle (tube) and push the icing to the end. Use the icing to pipe round the outline of the individual wings. Loosen up some of the icing with a few drops of water so that it is the consistency of double (whipping) cream. Carefully fill in the wings with this mixture, and leave to dry for 2–3 days. In addition, pipe two tiny strips on the acetate for each butterfly, which will be their antennae.

Make the cupcakes and fondant or ganache according to their recipe and ice the cakes. Let the icing dry.

Place the remaining royal icing (white or coloured) into a parchment piping bag and snip the end off the bag. This icing is going to be the body of the butterfly. Pipe quite a fat line down each cake, just longer than the inside wing of the butterfly. Pipe a little extra blob at the top for the head.

Extremely carefully, peel each wing off the acetate. You may find a small, flexible palette knife (metal spatula) helps here. Place each wing on the edge of the body you have just piped. If you can manage it, you can position the wings on the body at an angle so it looks as if they are about to take off. Trying not to mutter too much, peel off the antennae and stick them on the top of the butterfly's head. It's always worth making a few extra antennae in case they break ...

✻ TOP TIP:
Don't attempt these if you are in a hurry - you need to make the butterflies at least 2-3 days in advance.

Bollywood

There is a cake maker called Peggy Porschen who has been a huge influence on me. I love her work; it's witty, beautiful, very clever and her cakes look delicious. My Bollywood cakes are taken from an idea that I saw in her book *Pretty Party Cakes*. Her ideas about clashing colours, glitter and general over-the-topness hit all the right buttons. I salute her.

✳ Makes around 12

1 quantity of lemon cupcakes
   (see Lemonylicious p.32)
1 quantity of fondant icing
   (see p.19)
golf ball-sized piece of sugar
   paste (rolled fondant)
gel food colouring in assorted
   colours
cornflour (cornstarch)
   for dusting
1 tbsp royal icing (see p.17)
edible glitter (any colour to match
   your scheme, plus green for the
   leaves)
edible glue
edible lustre in gold
vodka

✳ *You will need 1 large and*
   1 small press-in rose mould,
   1 press-in leaf mould,
   2 parchment piping (decorat-
   ing) bags and a paintbrush

Decide on your colour scheme, and separate the sugar paste (rolled fondant) into four pieces. Using the gel food colouring, tint three of the pieces different reds or purples or whatever colours you want the flowers to be. Tint the fourth piece green. Knead in the colour so that each one is even.

Dust the moulds liberally with cornflour (cornstarch), and make 6 large roses, remembering to re-dust between pressing each flower. Continue the process, using the other moulds and dusting between each use, so that you end with 12 leaves and between 18 and 30 small flowers as well, depending on how committed you are!

Brush each rose lightly with edible glue and dust a little bit of glitter over each one. Do the same with the leaves with green glitter. Leave to dry out for around 24 hours.

Make the cupcakes as per the recipe on p.32, preferably in gold foil cupcake cases (baking cups) for the full-on Bollywood look. Remove from the oven and allow to cool. Meanwhile, make the fondant up following the method on p.19. Divide the mixture into as many bowls as you want colours. Really intensely colour the icing, making sure the

colour is even mixed in, and pour the icing onto the cakes. (The number of cakes you ice in each particular icing obviously depends on how many different colours you have.) Allow the icing to dry for at least 1 hour, preferably longer.

Carefully decide on your placement of the roses and stick to the cakes using edible glue. If you are using 2 leaves and a large rose, put the leaves on first, then the rose on top. If using the small flowers, decide whether you want three or five, and how you want them arranged before you commit yourself to gluing them in place.

Tint two-thirds of the royal icing the same green as the large leaves, and put into a parchment piping (decorating) bag with no nozzle. Squeeze the icing right to the end, then with very sharp scissors cut a small V shape out of the bottom of the bag. Practise piping on a work surface, and you will see that you are able to pipe tiny leaves. Dot a few of these around the small rose posies.

Next put the remaining white royal icing into a parchment piping bag, and snip just the very end off. Pipe small dots around the cakes, in groups or singly, as you wish. Leave to dry.

Mix a small amount of lustre on a saucer with a drop or two of vodka until you have a consistency like emulsion paint (quite thick). Carefully brush each of the white spots with the lustre. Allow them to dry.

They're done.

Women's essentials

I do believe that I am not the only female to show a passing interest in shoes, frocks and handbags. There is something rather wonderful about eating a cupcake adorned with a beautiful shoe. Not the same as actually buying a new pair and stroking them in their box, but cheaper. AND you don't have to go through the whole "Oh, no! I've had these for ages. Don't you remember?" routine.

✳ Makes about 12

1 quantity of lemon, basic vanilla or coffee cupcakes (see p.24, p.32 or p.33)
1 quantity of fondant icing (see p.19) (made with coffee if using coffee cakes)
2 tbsp royal icing (see p.17)
dark brown and pink gel food colouring

✳ *You will need two piping (decorating) bags with fine nozzles (tubes)*

Make the cupcakes in whichever recipe you choose. Allow to cool, then ice with pale pink fondant icing (or coffee fondant if using coffee cupcakes). Leave to dry for at least 1 hour.

Tint half the royal icing dark brown. If it gets too runny, add some more sifted icing (confectioners') sugar. Put the brown icing in a piping (decorating) bag with a fine nozzle (tube) and the remaining white royal icing into another one.

With the brown icing, pipe 1950-style dresses onto a few cakes (small waists, big skirts), high heeled shoes on a few more and handbags onto yet more. If you are stuck for ideas, look in a few magazines or draw out a few examples first. Fill in patterns and fold on the dresses, buckles and pockets on the bags, and stitch lines and other frivolities on the shoes with the white icing.

Paisley

This is one of those designs that translates really well into all colour schemes. I've made them in blue and pink pastels, lurid limes and purples, and quite autumnal browns and oranges. This means that they can be adapted to suit all ages, genders and occasions. Handy. They aren't tricky, but do require quite a few piping (decorating) bags on the go at any one time, hence their position in the high-faff section of the book.

✳ Makes about 12

1 quantity of lemon or basic vanilla cupcakes (see p.32 or p.24)
1 quantity of fondant icing (see p.68)
3 tbsp royal icing (see p.17)
gel food colouring in assorted colours

✳ *You will need 3 or 4 piping (decorating) bags with fine nozzles (tubes), depending on how many colours you wish to use*

Make the cupcakes according to whichever recipe you choose, and allow to cool.

Make the fondant icing and separate into three or four bowls and tint accordingly. Ice the cakes with the fondant icing and leave to dry for at least 1 hour.

Decide on the actual pattern you want to pipe. You can either go for it directly onto the cake or draw it out first. Start with a large, swirling paisley shape, then it's up to you. I think you need at least three colours within the pattern, and there needs to be outer embellishment and a distinct central part.

Very fanciful fondants

Fancy a fondant? The answer has to be yes. I will admit that these really are the high priestess of faff. But they're blooming lovely and I think worth pushing the boat out for. Don't make them for people who use food as fuel. I can't think of anything worse than someone scoffing one while talking about something entirely irrelevant and not even acknowledging that they are consuming your culinary slave labour. I'd cry.

✳ Makes about 16

sugar-paste (rolled fondant) roses, either rolled (see p.64) or pressed (p.76)
1 quantity of tray-bake recipe (see Basic Extremely Low-Faff Square Cakes p.29)
2 tbsp apricot jam
icing (confectioners') sugar for dusting
500 g/1 lb 2 oz marzipan
250 g/9 oz/2½ cups fondant sugar
juice of 1 lemon
food colouring (preferably gel)
edible glitter
edible glue
1 tbsp royal icing (see p.17)

✳ *You will need metallic foil cup-cake cases (baking cups) and a parchment piping (decorating) bag with a fine nozzle (tube)*

Make the roses a day before you want to make the cakes and leave them dry.

Make the tray-bake cake as per the recipe on p.29, and level off the top so that it is completely flat. Turn the cake upside down, so that the bottom is facing upwards. Warm the apricot jam and pass it through a sieve. Brush the top of the cake with a thin layer of jam.

Sprinkle some sifted icing (confectioners') sugar on a work surface, and roll out the marzipan until it is about 3 mm/⅛ in thick and the same size as the square sponge. Carefully lay the marzipan on top of the jam, and smooth over to get rid of any air pockets. Trim the edges of the cake, then cut it into four strips of equal width. Cut each strip in four, so that you end up with 16 squares.

Put the squares on a wire rack over a tray. Make up the fondant by combining the fondant sugar with the lemon juice, and colour it using the gel food colouring of your choice. Add a little more lemon juice or water if you need to – the consistency should be very thick, almost dough-like.

Gently warm the fondant over a pan of hot water, but don't overheat it. You want this fondant really quite runny, so you may wish to add even more liquid at this stage. It needs to be a tiny bit thicker than double (whipping) cream, but not cheese-sauce thick. Pour the icing over each cake so that it runs down the sides and creates an awful mess in the tray you have cunningly placed below. Leave to dry for a few minutes.

Once the fondant is dry enough, lay out your cupcake cases. Slightly dampen your fingers with a little water, then put the cakes in the cases and fold the cases round so that they stick to the cakes. When the cakes are completely dry (about 1 hour), stick the roses on with a drop of edible glue.

Tint some royal icing in the colour of your choice, and use to fill a piping (decorating) bag with a fine nozzle (tube). Pipe some spots or swirls around the cakes and leave to dry.

Floral faffdom

Clearly not the quickest way to make flowers, but I like the result. I don't think these are as difficult as the butterflies, but they are quite time-consuming. Great!

Makes about 12

white vegetable fat (vegetable shortening) such as Trex or Crisco
2 tbsp royal icing (see p.17) plus extra 1 scant tbsp for flower centres
food colouring (preferably gel)
1 quantity of cupcakes of your choice
1 quantity of fondant icing (see p.19) or chocolate ganache (see p.52) if you are using chocolate cakes
edible glue

You will need a sheet of clear acetate, a couple of parchment piping (decorating) bags and a fine paintbrush

You will find these pictured on p.75.

Cover a sheet of paper with petal templates (and leaves if you want to do leaves, too). Place the acetate over the paper, and wipe over a very thin layer of white vegetable fat.Decide what colour you want the flowers to be, and colour the 2 tbsp royal icing accordingly. Using a parchment piping (decorating) bag with the very end snipped off, pipe round the edges of the petals and leaves.

Thin out the rest of the coloured icing with a little water until it is the consistency of double (whipping) cream and carefully fill in the petals and leaves. Leave to dry for 2 or 3 days at least.

Make the cupcakes in whichever recipe you choose. Allow to cool, then cover with fondant icing or chocolate ganache as required. Let the icing or ganache dry completely.

Very carefully peel off the dry petals from the acetate, and stick them to the cakes with a tiny blob of edible glue under each petal. You may choose to have one flower per cake or a veritable posy. Add leaves as required.

Colour the small amount of extra royal icing whatever colour you want the centre of the flowers to be. Using a parchment piping bag with the very end snipped off, pipe a small blob into the centre of each flower and leave to dry.

Piped Easter eggs

Mildly spiced sponge cakes decorated with Easter eggs make a fine Easter treat – if you don't like the sound of the sponge, just make them with vanilla or lemon cupcakes instead.

✱ Makes about 12

110 g/4 oz/1 cup self-raising flour
110 g/4 oz/½ cup golden caster
  (superfine) sugar
1 tsp baking powder
½ tsp mixed spice or pumpkin
  pie spice
½ tsp freshly ground nutmeg
110 g/4 oz/½ cup margarine,
  softened
2 large free-range eggs
grated zest of 1 unwaxed lemon
1 quantity of fondant or glacé
  icing made with lemon juice or
  water (see p.19 or p.17)
food colouring (preferably gel)
2 tbsp royal icing (see p.17)
dragees (optional)

✱ *You will need several piping
(decorating) bags with fine
nozzles (tubes)*

Preheat the oven to 160°C/325°F/Gas mark 3. Line a 12-hole muffin tin (pan) with cupcake cases (baking cups).

Sift the flour, sugar, baking powder and spices into a large bowl, food processor or mixer. Add the margarine, eggs and lemon zest, and beat until light and fluffy. Scrape the sides of the bowl to make sure all the lemon and spices are being mixed in, and beat again for a few moments. Spoon the mixture (batter) into the prepared cases, and bake in the oven for 20 minutes until firm to the touch and golden. Remove from the oven and allow to cool.

Make the fondant or glacé icing, and tint whatever colour you like with the food colouring (don't feel you have to stick to pastels). If using the fondant, warm slightly over a double boiler. Ice the cakes and leave to dry.

Tint the royal icing into as many colours as you like, and start piping wildly patterned Easter eggs onto the cakes using piping (decorating) bags fitted with fine nozzles (tubes). Add dragees for extra sparkle, if you like.

Chocolate Easter eggs

We're on to chocolate here. No-holds-barred chocolate eggs on chocolate icing on chocolate cake. These are very good news in that they are a) easy, b) look fantastic, c) give you the opportunity for some serious bowl licking, and d) taste delicious. If you are feeling an extra-chocolatey yen, make them with Choc-a-doodle-do cupcakes (see p.52).

✳ Makes about 12

1 quantity of chocolate cupcakes
   (see p.35)
1 quantity of chocolate ganache
   (see p.52)
36 coloured chocolate mini
   Easter eggs

Make the cupcakes as per the recipe on p.35, and allow them to cool.

Make the chocolate ganache as per the recipe on p.52, and spoon over the cakes. Let them dry for just a few minutes. Before the ganache is completely set, pop 3 eggs onto each cake. Leave them to set for a few hours before scoffing.

Chirpy chirpy cheep cheep

I love those little fluffy yellow chicks that appear in shops just before Easter. If you don't want to do anything other than ice some cupcakes, you could stand one of these chicks on top. Just make sure that no one thinks that they are edible. Otherwise these simple piped chicks look very lovely. Pastel colours really do look better here.

Makes about 12

1 quantity of basic vanilla or spiced cupcakes (see p.24 or p.85)
1 quantity of fondant or glacé icing (see p.19 or p.17) tinted in pastel colours with gel food colouring
2 tbsp royal icing (see p.17) plus 1 tbsp green royal icing (optional)
yellow, black and orange gel food colouring

You will need 3 piping (decorating) bags with fine nozzles (tubes)

Make the cupcakes and allow them to cool. Ice the cooled cupcakes with a selection of pastel-coloured icings in glacé or fondant. Leave them to dry.

Split the royal icing into thirds. Take two-thirds and tint it yellow with gel food colouring. Fill a piping (decorating) bag with the yellow icing, and push to the end. To make a fluffy chick, pipe a chick shape onto the cake, and fill in the chick with random squiggles of yellow icing. Make sure that you go ever so slightly over your outline, so that the chick looks really fluffy. To make a flatter chick, again pipe an outline. Thin out some of the yellow royal icing with a few drops of water so that you have a consistency a bit thicker than double (whipping) cream. Carefully fill in the outline with this mixture, and leave to dry completely.

When both are dry, divide the remaining royal icing into two, and tint one portion black and the other orange. Fill two separate piping bags, one with the black and one with the orange. Pipe an eye on each chick (two if the chick is not in profile!) with the black icing, and a beak with the orange.

If you have any extra royal icing, tint it another colour (green looks good), and pipe tiny spots all the way round the outer edge of the cake.

Gadzooks for the spooks

Black Halloween cupcakes are highly entertaining. Black icing is wonderful – it transforms your teeth and mouth at first bite. There is absolutely no room for subtlety here. You can scare the living daylights out of trick-or-treaters, by having a mouthful of cake just before you open the door. Rest assured that the colour does fade quite rapidly ...

✳ Makes about 12

1 quantity of lemon or basic
   vanilla cupcakes (see p.32
   or p.24)
1 quantity of glacé or fondant
   icing (see p.17 or p.19)
black and orange food colouring
   (preferably gel)
golf ball-sized piece of sugar
   paste (rolled fondant)
edible glue

✳ *You will need a small
   paintbrush*

Make the cupcakes and allow to cool. Make up the glacé or fondant icing, and divide into two portions; use the food colouring to make one black and the other deep orange. Divide the cupcakes into two batches, and ice one batch black and the other batch orange. Leave them to dry. (These cakes need to be completely dry before you add anything else because of the dark colours.)

Take a third of the sugar paste (rolled fondant) and tint it black. Make a ghost by flattening out a piece of white sugar paste into the shape of a ghost and use edible glue to stick it onto a black-iced cupcake. Let the ghost trail over the edge of the cake in a ghostly manner. Take some tiny bits of black paste, and stick them on to make a ghoulish face for the ghost.

Make the spider by taking a bit of black paste the size of a broad (fava) bean, and sticking it onto an orange-iced cake using edible glue. Make as many legs as you can (8 is traditional!) out of slivers of black paste, and stick them on. I also like to add a final strip of black for the web. A face and fangs made out of white sugar paste finishes it off.

For the spooky eyes, take 2 elongated egg shapes of white paste, add black pupils and stick onto a black-iced cake.

Firework frenzy

Is it just me or are more people having their own firework parties these days? Much as I enjoy a municipal gathering where thousands of huge fireworks are let off in spectacularly successful fashion, there is a part of me that hankers after a few unpredictable rockets zooming off into next door's garden. The inevitable pause between fireworks is always a good moment to get some food out. Sausages? Yes. Baked potatoes? Yes. Cupcakes? Definitely. Should you be of a nervous disposition and shy away from explosive devices, never fear. Stick a small, indoor sparkler into the top of the cake, turn the lights out and behold the gentle fizzing.

✳ Makes about 12

1 quantity of any sort of
   cupcakes
1 quantity of fondant or glacé
   icing (see p.19 or p.17) or
   chocolate ganache (see p.52)
gel food colourings
2 tbsp royal icing (see p.17)
dragees (multicoloured if
   possible)
edible glitter (optional)

✳ *You will need 3 or 4 piping
(decorating) bags with fine
nozzles (tubes)*

Make the cakes as for whichever recipe you choose, and make up the icing appropriate to the cake.

Ice the cakes – if not using chocolate, a really deep navy icing seems best to imitate the night sky. Let the icing dry really well (including the ganache).

Separate the royal icing into as many bowls as you want colours, and tint them accordingly with the food colouring. Using piping (decorating) bags with fine nozzles (tubes), pipe on whatever firework takes your fancy – Catherine wheels, rockets, shooting stars and those amazing fountains of coloured baubles all go well.

Sprinkle a tiny bit of edible glitter over them if you wish, and run free with the dragees, which may need a tiny dab of royal icing underneath them to hold them in place.

Sparkling Christmas trees

This is really easy if you have a Christmas tree cutter.
If you haven't, just cut them out freehand.

✳ Makes about 12

110 g/4 oz/½ cup butter,
    softened
110 g/4 oz/½ cup caster
    (superfine) sugar
2 large free-range eggs
110 g/4 oz/1 cup self-raising flour
½ tsp ground cinnamon
½ tsp ground cloves
½ tsp ground nutmeg
½ tsp ground ginger
1 tbsp milk (if needed)
1 quantity of fondant icing made
    with lemon juice (see p.19)
gel food colouring (optional)
cornflour (cornstarch)
    for dusting
golf ball-sized piece of sugar
    paste (rolled fondant)
edible glue
edible glitter

Preheat the oven to 160°C/325°F/Gas mark 3. Line a 12-hole muffin tin (pan) with cupcake cases (baking cups).

Cream the butter and sugar together until really pale and fluffy. Beat the eggs in a separate bowl, and slowly add them to the butter and sugar mixture, beating well between each addition. Sift the flour, baking powder and spices onto the mixture, and carefully fold it all in using a large metal spoon. If the mixture (batter) doesn't gently plop off a spoon, add the milk and stir in. Spoon into the prepared cases, and bake in the oven for around 20 minutes until firm to the touch and golden. Remove from the oven and allow to cool.

Once the cupcakes have cooled, cover with the lemon fondant icing (whatever colour you like, but white looks nice and snowy). Let the icing dry.

Dust a work surface with cornflour (cornstarch), and roll out the sugar paste (rolled fondant) to about 3 mm/⅛ in thick. Cut out 12 Christmas trees, either using a Christmas tree cutter or freehand.

Paint a thin layer of edible glue carefully over the entire tree, and dip the tree in glitter. Put a little blob of edible glue onto the middle of the cake and carefully place the tree onto the cake. Continue until you have a tree on each of your cupcakes. Leave to dry.

Snowflake cupcakes

These are very pretty and can be jazzed up with the judicious use of dragees if a little sparkle is wanted. I really like these made with almond cupcakes – not sure why, but they just seem right.

Makes about 12

1 quantity of almond cupcakes
   (see Bite My Cherry p.49)
1 quantity of fondant icing made
   with lemon juice (see p.19)
pale blue food colouring
   (preferably gel)
2 tbsp royal icing (see p.17)
silver dragees (optional)

*You will need 2 piping
(decorating) bags with fine
nozzles (tubes)*

Make the cupcakes according to the recipe on p.49 (omitting the cherry, unless you particularly want it), and allow them to cool.

Make the fondant icing and divide it into two bowls. Tint one bowl very pale blue, and ice six cupcakes blue and six white. Let the icing dry.

Divide the royal icing into two bowls, and tint one bowl the same blue as the fondant icing. Using two separate piping (decorating) bags with fine nozzles (tubes), pipe white snowflakes onto the blue cakes and blue snowflakes onto the white cakes. If your piping is a bit random, console your-self with the fact that no two snowflakes are the same. Add silver dragees to the centre and the ends of the snowflakes, if wished. Leave to dry.

Fruitcake

Calm down. It's not the fruitcake that you are thinking of – these are light and spongy and don't require two hands to lift one off a plate. This recipe is a spicy sponge, much like the recipe for Sparkling Christmas Trees (see p.94), but with the addition of some rum-soaked raisins and a few glacé (candied) cherries. I have piped Christmas trees on top of these, but you could add whatever you wished.

✳ Makes about 12

110 g/4 oz/½ cup butter, softened
110 g/4 oz/½ cup golden caster (superfine) sugar
2 large free-range eggs
110 g/4 oz/1 cup self-raising flour
1 tsp baking powder
½ tsp mixed spice or pumpkin pie spice
50 g/1¾ oz/⅓ cup raisins, soaked in rum or brandy for 1 hour, drained
18 glacé (candied) cherries, quartered
1 tbsp milk (if needed)
1 quantity of fondant icing made with lemon juice (see p.19)
2 tbsp royal icing (see p.17)
silver dragees

✳ *You will need a piping (decorating) bag fitted with a fine nozzle (tube)*

Preheat the oven to 160°C/325°F/Gas mark 3. Line a 12-hole muffin tin (pan) with cupcake cases (baking cups).

Cream butter and sugar together until pale and fluffy. Beat the eggs in a separate bowl, and gradually add to the butter and sugar mixture, beating well between each addition. Add the drained soaked raisins and beat well.

Sift the flour, baking powder and mixed spice onto a large plate, and toss the quartered cherries into the flour. Carefully add to the wet mixture, and fold in with a large metal spoon. If the mixture is a little dry, add the milk, so that the mixture (batter) plops gently off a spoon. Spoon carefully into the prepared cases, and bake in the oven for 20 minutes until firm to the touch and golden. Remove from the oven and allow to cool.

Once the cupcakes have cooled, make up the fondant icing and use to ice the cupcakes. Leave to dry.

Put the royal icing into a piping (decorating) bag, and pipe Christmas tree shapes onto the cakes. Add silver dragees to the trees as decorations.

Twinkle, twinkle

Christmas, stars, glitter – they all go together so beautifully it would be insane not to have them here on a cupcake. I've used lemon cupcakes here, but it's not 100 per cent necessary. Up to you.

* Makes about 12

110 g/4 oz/½ cup butter, softened
110 g/4 oz/½ cup caster (superfine) sugar
2 large free-range eggs
grated zest and juice of 1 large unwaxed lemon
110 g/4 oz/1 cup self-raising flour
1 tsp baking powder
1 quantity of fondant icing made with lemon juice (see p.19)
cornflour (cornstarch) for dusting
golf ball-sized piece of sugar paste (rolled fondant)
edible glue
edible glitter in silver and gold

You will need a star-shaped cutter and a paintbrush

Preheat the oven to 160°C/325°F/Gas mark 3. Line a 12-hole muffin tin (pan) with cupcake cases (baking cups).

Cream the butter and sugar together until really pale and fluffy. Beat the eggs in a separate bowl, and gradually add them to the butter and sugar mixture, beating well between each addition. Add the lemon zest and beat well.

Sift in the flour and baking powder, and fold in with a large metal spoon. If the mixture (batter) needs loosening a bit, add a little lemon juice. The mixture should gently plop off a spoon. Spoon the mixture into the prepared cases, and bake in the oven for 20 minutes until firm to the touch and golden. Remove from the oven and allow to cool.

Once cool, make the fondant icing and use to ice the cupcakes. Leave to dry.

Dust a work surface with cornflour (cornstarch), and roll out the sugar paste (rolled fondant) until it is about 3 mm/⅛ in thick. Cut out 12 star shapes using a star-shaped cutter.

Paint edible glue over each star, making sure they are completely covered, before dipping 6 stars in gold glitter and 6 in silver glitter. Dab a tiny blob of edible glue on the centre of each cupcake and carefully place a star on top.

White Christmas

These have got to be the ultimate in good taste. No colour and a tiny smidgen of silver. I wish I could hate them, but I don't. The marzipan addition is completely optional.

※ Makes around 12

1 quantity of lemon cupcakes
  (see Twinkle Twinkle, opposite)
350 g/12 oz marzipan
icing (confectioners') sugar for
  dusting
2 tbsp apricot jam
1 quantity of fondant icing made
  with lemon juice (see p.19)
cornflour (cornstarch) for
  dusting
golf ball-sized piece of sugar
  paste (rolled fondant)
edible glue
silver dragees

※ *You will need 2 star-shaped*
  cutters, one smaller than
  the other, and a round cutter
  the same size as your
  lemon cupcakes

Make the cupcakes and allow them to cool.

Put the apricot jam into a small saucepan and warm over a gentle heat, then push the jam through a fine sieve to remove any lumps. Brush the jam over the cakes.

Sprinkle some icing (confectioners') sugar over a work surface, and roll out the marzipan to about 3 mm/⅛ in thick. Using a round cutter the same diameter as the top of your cupcakes, cut out 12 circles and place them carefully on top of the jam.

Make the fondant icing and pour on top of the marzipan. Leave to dry thoroughly.

Lightly dust a work surface with cornflour (cornstarch) and roll out the sugar paste (rolled fondant) until it is about 3 mm/⅛ in thick. Cut out 12 large stars and 12 smaller stars.

When the fondant is dry, put a tiny dab of edible glue on the centre of each cake and place a large star on top. Then put a dab of glue on the centre of the star and place the smaller star on top.

With a cocktail stick (toothpick) make a little indent in the centre of the top star and, again with the cocktail stick, apply a smidgen of edible glue. Carefully put one silver dragee into this little indent.

Chocolate mince pies

Bitterness is the key here. I know it sounds wrong, but mincemeat is so sweet that 100% cacao is the perfect foil (100% cacao is quite widely available but, if you can't find it, use the most bitter chocolate you can find). You will have some mincemeat left over; put it in a jar and store in the refrigerator.

✳ Makes 12

For the chocolate pastry
50 g/1¾ oz/scant ½ stick butter
50 g/1¾ oz/scant ¼ cup lard or white vegetable fat (shortening)
200 g/7 oz/1⅓ cups plain (all-purpose) flour
25 g/1 oz/¼ cup cocoa powder (unsweetened cocoa)
25 g/1 oz/⅛ cup caster (superfine) sugar
1 large egg yolk
1 large egg, beaten, for egg wash

For the mincemeat
100 ml/3½ fl oz/scant ½ cup apple juice
100 g/3½ oz/½ cup (solidly packed) soft dark brown sugar
450 g/1 lb cooking apples, peeled, cored and chopped
100 g/3½ oz/⅔ cup currants
100 g/3½ oz/⅔ cup sultanas (golden raisins)
50 g /1¾ oz/½ cup flaked (slivered) almonds
1 tsp ground cinnamon
1 tsp allspice
½ tsp ground cloves
50 g/1¾ oz 100% cacao, grated

First make the pastry: in a food processor, blitz the butter, lard (shortening), flour, cocoa and sugar until the mixture resembles fine breadcrumbs. Add the egg yolk and blitz again. If the dough does not come together, add cold water 1 teaspoon at a time. When you have a ball of dough, wrap it in clingfilm (plastic wrap) and pop it into the refrigerator.

Put the apple juice and the sugar into a big saucepan and heat until the sugar has dissolved. Add the remaining ingredients and gently bubble away for 25–30 minutes, or until the apples have cooked and you have the most wonderful, dark, fragrant mixture. Be careful that it doesn't stick to the pan. If you need to add more apple juice, do so.

Preheat the oven to 180°C/350°F/Gas Mark 4 and take the pastry out of the refrigerator. Give it a quick knead on a floured surface and then roll out until about 3 mm/⅛ in thick. Cut out circles and place them into a greased 12-hole bun tin (pan). Re-roll the remaining pastry and cut out 12 small stars. Put a teaspoonful of mincemeat into each pastry case and top with a pastry star. Brush a little bit of egg wash onto the star and then bake in the oven for 15 minutes, or until the pastry is crisp.

Delicious hot, with ice cream, or brandy butter, or cold.

Mum's brownies

Please be aware of the honour that is being bestowed upon you. My mother makes excellent brownies. She puts chopped nuts in hers – I don't. Up to you. They're delicious either way.

✳ Makes about 16

110 g/4 oz/1 stick butter
50 g/1¾ oz/1¾ squares plain (bittersweet) chocolate (70% cocoa solids), broken into large chunks
2 large eggs, lightly beaten
225 g/8 oz/1⅛ cups caster (superfine) sugar
50 g/1¾ oz/⅓ cup plain flour, sifted
1 tsp baking powder
100 g/3½ oz/⅔ cup chopped nuts (optional)
pinch of salt

Preheat the oven to 180°C/350°F/Gas Mark 4 and line a tin (pan) with greaseproof (waxed) paper. Leave the paper about 5 cm/2 in above the height of the tin, because the brownie rises before it falls.

Melt the butter and the chocolate in a heatproof bowl over a pan of barely simmering water – don't let the bottom of the bowl touch the water. When it has melted and is lovely and smooth, take it off the heat and let it cool slightly for a few minutes. Then add the remaining ingredients and beat well. Spread the mixture into the tin and flatten it out.

Bake for 30 minutes. The top should have crusted over, but the innards should still be moist. The brownie will continue to solidify as it cools. Have faith! There is nothing worse than an overcooked brownie.

Leave the brownie in the tin to cool before cutting and then transfer to a wire rack to cool completely.

Blondies

Well, if Mum's Brownies (p.103) are the classic brownie, then these are the great interlopers, coming up from behind and giving you a great big kiss on the chops. This is a recipe with a "more is more" approach. Nuts? Yes, bung them in. White chocolate? Oh, yes please. Chocolate chips too? Absolutely essential. I like to think of them as the Versace of the brownie world, darling.

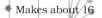 Makes about 16

110 g/4 oz/1 stick butter
250 g/9 oz/9 squares white
    chocolate, broken into chunks
2 large eggs, lightly beaten
50 g/1¾ oz/¼ cup caster
    (superfine) sugar
2 tsp vanilla extract
125 g/4 ½ oz/generous ⅔ cup
    plain (all-purpose) flour, sifted
100 g/3 ½ oz/generous ½ cup
    plain (bittersweet) chocolate
    chips
100 g/3 ½ oz/⅔ cup hazelnuts,
    roasted and chopped

Preheat the oven to 180°C/350°F/Gas Mark 4. Line a 20 cm/8 in square tin (pan) with greaseproof (waxed) paper, or a silicone liner, and leave about 5 cm/2 in poking up over the top of the tin.

In a heatproof bowl over a pan of barely simmering water, melt the butter and 125 g/4½ oz/4½ squares of the white chocolate. Don't let the bottom of the bowl touch the water. When it has melted, take it off the heat and stir in the rest of the white chocolate. Keep stirring. The residual heat will melt it. Leave to one side for a few moments to cool slightly.

In another bowl, whisk the eggs and sugar together until pale and thick. Add the chocolate and butter mixture, the vanilla and flour, then beat thoroughly but quickly. Add the chocolate chips and nuts and stir until evenly mixed.

Pour into the tin and smooth the top. Bake for 30 minutes, or until crusted and golden on top and still squidgy in the middle. Leave it all to cool in the tin, then cut into squares.

Chocolate Guinness cake

At the market the other day, I met a man who said he didn't like chocolate. Determined not to let this pass, I started telling him about Chocolate and Guinness cake. Well, I changed his mind.

Serves 8

110 g/4 oz/1 stick butter, softened
275 g/9½ oz/generous 1⅓ cups (solidly packed) light soft brown sugar
2 large eggs, lightly beaten
200 ml/7 fl oz/generous ¾ cup Guinness
175 g/6 oz/scant 1¼ cups plain (all-purpose) flour, sifted
50 g/1¾ oz/½ cup cocoa powder (unsweetened cocoa)
1 tsp bicarbonate of soda (baking soda)
½ tsp cream of tartar

Preheat the oven to 180°C/350°F/Gas Mark 4. Line a 450 g/1 lb loaf tin (pan) – I use one of those ready-made fluted loaf liners.

Cream the butter and sugar until pale and fluffy and then beat in the eggs a little bit at a time. Add the Guinness and stir well. Add the flour, cocoa, bicarbonate of soda (baking soda) and cream of tartar. (I find it easiest to put all these dry ingredients into a sieve/strainer over the bowl and sift it straight into the bowl.) Carefully fold the dry ingredients into the wet and then pour into the prepared tin. Bake for 40–45 minutes, or until a skewer comes out clean. If the cake looks like it is getting a bit overdone on top, cover it with some greaseproof (waxed) paper while it finishes cooking.

I don't think this cake requires any form of icing – it is gorgeous just cut into manly slabs.

Basic chocolate cake

This is a cake to make when you have people coming to tea and you want to impress but don't have the time or inclination to take any risks or expend any effort with twiddles and twirls. The combination of chocolate and blackcurrant is gorgeous. The cake looks lovely and is one of those recipes that you can pull out when you don't know what else to do. It is the cake equivalent of the little black dress.

❋ Serves 8

150 g/5½ oz/1 cup self-raising (self-rising) flour, sifted
25 g/1 oz/¼ cup cocoa powder (unsweetened cocoa)
175 g/6 oz/scant 1 cup caster (superfine) sugar
175 g/6 oz/¾ cup soft margarine
3 large eggs
1 tsp vanilla extract
200 ml/7 fl oz/generous ¾ cup double (heavy) cream
2 tbsp blackcurrant jam (jelly)
icing (confectioners') sugar, for dusting

Preheat the oven to 180°C/350°F/Gas Mark 4. Butter and line two 20 cm/8 in cake tins (pans) with greaseproof (waxed) paper.

In a mixer, food processor, or large bowl with an electric hand whisk, beat together the flour, cocoa, sugar, margarine, eggs and vanilla until light brown and really fluffy. (I said it was basic.)

Split the mixture between the two tins and smooth out. Bake for 25 minutes, or until the cake top is springy to the touch and a skewer stuck into the middle of the cake comes out clean.

Turn the cakes onto a wire rack to cool and remove the greaseproof paper.

When the cakes are cold, whisk the cream until it reaches soft peaks. Try not to overwhip it. Spread the jam (jelly) over one of the cakes and then top with the cream. Place the other cake on top and dust the very top with icing (confectioners') sugar.

Chocolate fudge cake

If you are after a rich, moist chocolate cake with a fudgy, truffle-y icing, then this is the bad boy for you.

✱ Serves 8

175 g/6 oz/1¼ sticks butter, softened
350 g/12 oz/1¾ cups caster (superfine) sugar
1 tsp vanilla extract
3 large eggs
175 ml/6 fl oz/¾ cup milk
5 tbsp sour cream
75 g/2¾ oz/½ cup plain (all-purpose) flour, sifted
150 g/5½ oz/1 cup self-raising (self-rising) flour
100 g/3½ oz/1 cup cocoa powder (unsweetened cocoa)
2 tbsp Nutella, or other chocolate spread

For the icing
200 ml/7 fl oz/generous ¾ cup double (heavy) cream
200 g/7 oz/7 squares plain (bittersweet) chocolate (70% cocoa solids), broken into gravel-sized pieces

✱ *You will need a 20 cm/8 in loose-based cake tin (pan)*

Preheat the oven to 180°C/350°F/Gas Mark 4. Butter and line the cake tin (pan) with greaseproof (waxed) paper.

In a large bowl, beat the butter, sugar and vanilla together until light and fluffy. Add the eggs, one at a time, beating well between each addition. Now add the milk and sour cream and beat away. You will think it's curdled, but don't worry! Sift over the mixture both the flours and the cocoa, then fold in. Pop the mixture into the tin, smooth it down, and make a slight dent in the centre of the cake with the back of a spoon. Bake for 1 hour, or until a skewer poked into the middle of the cake comes out clean. You may need to cover the top of the cake with baking paper (parchment paper) for the last 10 minutes or so, if it looks like the top is burning. Remove the cake from the oven and leave to cool for 10 minutes in its tin, then turn onto a wire rack to cool.

Prepare the ganache for the icing. Heat the cream in a heavy-based pan until just below boiling point. Take it off the heat and let any bubbles die away, then tip in the chocolate and stir gently until it has all melted and you are left with a shiny ganache. Leave to cool and thicken for 10 minutes.

Cut the cake horizontally through the middle and sandwich together with the Nutella. Place the cake on the wire rack over a tray. Pour the ganache over the whole cake, then use a palette knife (spatula) to spread it all over the top and round the sides. Leave it well alone to firm up and set for at least 1 hour before serving.

Beet the choccy cake

Before you turn your nose up at this, may I point out that dyed-in-the-wool beet haters (husband and son) have no trouble at all eating this like it's going out of fashion. I made this recipe into cupcakes and took a huge batch to my local farmers' market, and they positively flew! There is something deliciously satisfying about the rich and moist sponge, which is intensely chocolatey but with a fruity undertone. The chocolate cream cheese frosting isn't too bad, either.

✳ Serves 8

150 g/5½ oz raw beetroot (beet), grated
200 ml/7 fl oz/generous ¾ cup sunflower (corn) oil
250 g/9 oz/1¼ cups caster (superfine) sugar
3 large eggs, separated
3 tbsp milk
2 tsp chocolate extract (optional)
200 g/7 oz/1⅓ cups self-raising (self-rising) flour
1 heaped tbsp cocoa powder (unsweetened cocoa)
1 tsp baking powder

For the frosting
50 g/1¾ oz/1¾ squares plain (bittersweet) chocolate
250 g/9 oz/generous 1 cup cream cheese
300 g/10½ oz/3 cups icing (confectioners') sugar, sifted

Preheat the oven to 170°C/325°F/Gas Mark 3 and grease and line two 20 cm/8 in cake tins (pans).

Take a small spoonful of the grated beetroot (beet) and pop it in a bowl and then just cover with boiling water. Set aside.

Whisk together the oil and sugar, then add the egg yolks, one by one, whisking well between each addition. Add the milk and the chocolate extract (if using) and carry on whisking. Stir in the remaining grated beetroot. Sift in the flour, cocoa and baking powder and fold that in too.

In another bowl, whisk the egg white until really stiff and then fold into the mixture in three batches.

Divide the mixture between the two tins and bake for 30 minutes, or until a skewer comes out clean. Leave the cakes in the tins to cool for about 5 minutes, then turn out onto a wire rack to cool completely.

To make the frosting, melt the chocolate according to your preferred method, then leave to cool. Put the cream cheese and icing (confectioners') sugar into a big bowl and beat well and icing (confectioners') sugar into a big bowl and beat well until smooth. Add the melted chocolate and stir it in.

From the bowl containing the beetroot and water, take 1 teaspoon of the intensely coloured liquid and add it to the frosting. If you find that this has made the frosting too runny, add a bit more icing sugar.

When the cakes are cold, take about one-third of the frosting and sandwich the two cakes together. Then use the remaining frosting to cover the top and the sides of the cake. A palette knife (spatula) will make your life much easier here. Decorate the cake with chocolate sprinkles, Maltesers or a bit of grated chocolate. Not necessary, but always welcome.

Leave the cake for 1–2 hours before serving.

Chocolate mousse cake

Oh hello, you sophisticated little number! Look at you there, looking all simple and un-fussed about with. But what darkness lies beneath? Something rather sinfully unctuous, that's what. This recipe is a classic example of why they tell you, "Don't judge a book by its cover". Plain at first glance – but one spoonful, and you are doomed. You can serve this with cream and some fruit, but it is lovely by itself.

✳ Serves 6

250 g/9 oz/9 squares plain
   (bittersweet) chocolate
4 large eggs, separated
110 g/4 oz/generous ½ cup
   caster (superfine) sugar
3 tbsp warmish water
cocoa powder (unsweetened
   cocoa), for dusting

Preheat the oven to 180°C/350°F/Gas Mark 4. Grease a 20 cm/8 in loose-based cake tin (pan) and then line the base with greaseproof (waxed) paper.

Melt the chocolate according to your preferred method, then let it cool slightly. Whisk together the egg yolks and the sugar until really pale and fluffy. (I use an electric whisk for this, but an ordinary one will do, though it will take a bit of time.) Carefully stir in the chocolate and the water.

In another bowl, whisk the egg whites until they form soft peaks and then fold them into the chocolate mixture, a third at a time.

Pour the mixture into the prepared tin and bake for 15 minutes. Take it out of the oven and leave it to cool, then chill in the refrigerator for at least 2 hours – overnight is better.

Take it out of the refrigerator 1 hour before serving. It slides out of the tin easily, but use a hot, wet knife to slice cleanly. Dust heavily with cocoa powder (unsweetened cocoa) for a sophisticated look.

Chocolate brandy cake

I used to work in a magical café in Exeter. Sadly, it doesn't exist anymore. There was a gaggle of us girls who used to whip up concoctions amid much laughter and scandalous gossip. This refrigerator cake was a café favourite. It is delicious and easy, freezes well, and always hits the spot. Who could ask for more?

✳ Serves 12

250 g/9 oz/9 squares plain (bittersweet) chocolate
225 g/8 oz/2 sticks butter
3 large eggs
75 g/2 ¾ oz/generous ⅓ cup soft light brown sugar
225 g/8 oz digestive biscuits, crushed
175 g/6 oz/generous 1 cup raisins, soaked in 3 tbsp brandy for 1 hour
100 ml/3 ½ fl oz/scant ½ cup double (heavy) cream
100 g/3 ½ oz/3 ½ squares plain (bittersweet) chocolate, chopped into pieces

Line the base of a large flan dish, preferably one with a removable base.

Melt the chocolate and butter together in a heatproof bowl over a pan of barely simmering water. Don't let the bottom of the bowl touch the water. When melted, set to one side.

In a very large bowl, whisk the eggs and sugar together until really pale and fluffy. (It really pays to go for it here: use an electrical whisk and save your arms.) When you are happy with the pale fluffiness, add the chocolate and butter mixture, the crushed biscuits and the raisins and any brandy still sloshing in the bottom of the bowl. Stir well to combine.

Pour the mixture into the lined dish and smooth it out and press down slightly with the back of a spoon. Cover with clingfilm (plastic wrap) and then either pop it straight into the freezer for another day, or stick it in the refrigerator for about 3 hours to firm up. About 1 hour before serving, take it out of the refrigerator and pop onto a serving plate.

Heat the cream in a heavy-based saucepan. Remove from the heat just before it comes to the boil, then add the chocolate. Stir until the chocolate has melted and you have a lovely, smooth, shiny ganache. Pour over the top of the cake and leave to set. Yummy. (If you prefer a plainer cake, simply dust with icing (confectioners') sugar instead.)

muffins

Coconut-lime muffins

For the truly faff-free muffin, you can serve these little beauties just as they are, still warm from the oven. But for the ultimate limey, coconutty, creamy experience, go the whole mile and serve them with lashings of cream cheese frosting and piles of snowy-white coconut shavings.

✳ Makes 12

300 g/10 oz/2 cups self-raising flour
1 tsp baking powder
150 g/5 oz/⅔ cup caster sugar
1 egg, beaten
200 ml/7 fl oz/generous ¾ cup coconut milk
grated zest of 2 limes
100 ml/3½ fl oz/scant ½ cup sunflower oil
50 g/1¾ oz/½ cup desiccated coconut

To decorate
150 g/5 oz cream cheese
50 g/1¾ oz/⅓ cup icing sugar
2 tsp lime juice
coconut shavings, for sprinkling

Preheat the oven to 200°C/400°F/Gas 6. Grease or line a 12-hole muffin pan.

Combine the flour, baking powder and caster sugar and sift into a large bowl.

In a separate bowl or jug, combine the egg, coconut milk, lime zest and juice, oil and desiccated coconut, then pour into the dry ingredients. Stir together until just combined, then spoon big dollops of the mixture into the prepared muffin pan.

Bake for about 20 minutes until risen and golden. Leave to cool in the pan for a couple of minutes, then transfer to a wire rack to cool.

To serve, beat together the cream cheese, icing sugar and lime juice until smooth and creamy. Swirl on top of the muffins and sprinkle with coconut shavings.

Apple muffins with cinnamon butter

Throw together a batch of these comforting muffins and find your kitchen filled with the sweet smell of cinnamon. For a faff-free but to-die-for twist, serve them still warm, broken open and smeared with melting cinnamon butter.

✱ Makes 12

300 g/10 oz/2 cups self-raising flour
½ tsp bicarbonate of soda
1 tsp ground cinnamon
2 eggs, beaten
75 ml/3 fl oz/scant ⅓ cup plain yogurt
100 ml/3½ fl oz/scant ½ cup milk
115 g/4 oz/½ cup soft brown sugar
6 tbsp sunflower oil
2 apples, peeled, cored and finely diced

For the cinnamon butter
115 g/4 oz butter, at room temperature
60 g/2 oz/⅓ cup icing sugar, sifted
1 tsp ground cinnamon

Preheat the oven to 200°C/400°F/Gas 6. Grease or line a 12-hole muffin pan.

Combine the flour, bicarbonate of soda and cinnamon and sift into a large bowl.

In a separate bowl, combine the eggs, yogurt, milk, brown sugar and oil, then stir in the apples. Pour the mixture into the dry ingredients and stir together until just combined, then spoon big dollops of the mixture into the prepared muffin pan.

Bake for about 20 minutes until risen and golden. Leave to cool in the pan for a couple of minutes, then transfer to a wire rack to cool.

Meanwhile, beat together the butter, icing sugar and cinnamon. Serve the muffins warm, with the cinnamon butter for spreading.

Nutty banana and choc chip chomps

Throwing a handful of white chocolate chips into this old favourite adds a spot of wicked indulgence just where you need it. Eat them while they're still warm to really enjoy the oozing stickiness of the melted chocolate inside. Yum!

✳ Makes 12

300 g/10 oz/2 cups plain flour
1 tbsp baking powder
85 g/3 oz/scant ½ cup soft
   brown sugar
150 ml/5 fl oz/scant ⅔ cup milk
1 egg, beaten
100 ml/3½ fl oz/scant ½ cup
   sunflower oil
2 ripe bananas, roughly mashed
85 g/3 oz/⅔ cup walnut pieces
100 g/3½ oz white chocolate
   chips

Preheat the oven to 200°C/400°F/Gas 6. Grease or line a 12-hole muffin pan.

Combine the flour and baking powder and sift into a large bowl.

In a separate bowl, combine the sugar, milk, egg, oil and bananas, then stir in the nuts and chocolate chips and tip into the dry ingredients. Stir together until just combined, then spoon big dollops of the mixture into the prepared muffin pan.

Bake for about 20 minutes until risen and golden. Leave to cool in the pan for a few minutes, then transfer to a wire rack to cool.

Spotty dotty orange and poppy seed

Fresh, zesty and not too sweet, these little rascals are just right for a lazy weekend breakfast. Serve them warm with a mug of freshly brewed coffee, and if you're feeling extra-naughty, try them with a spoonful of crème fraîche and a dollop of orange curd on top.

✳ Makes 12

300 g/10 oz/2 cups plain flour
1 tbsp baking powder
115 g/4 oz/½ cup caster sugar
2 tbsp poppy seeds
1 egg, beaten
100 ml/3½ fl oz/generous ⅓ cup plain yogurt
3 tbsp milk
50 g/1¾ oz butter, melted
grated zest and juice of 2 oranges

✳ You will find these pictured on the front cover.

Preheat the oven to 200°C/400°F/Gas 6. Grease or line a 12-hole muffin pan.

Combine the flour, baking powder, sugar and poppy seeds and sift into a large bowl.

In a separate bowl or jug, lightly beat together the egg, yogurt and milk to combine, then stir in the butter and orange juice and zest. Pour into the dry ingredients and stir together until just combined, then spoon big dollops of the mixture into the prepared muffin pan.

Bake for about 20 minutes until risen and golden. Leave to cool in the pan for a few minutes, then transfer to a wire rack to cool.

Blueberry bliss

Is it those dark purply berries oozing juice, or the tender vanilla crumb that makes this classic such a favourite? Eat them still warm from the oven to enjoy them at their very best. This simple recipe is made without eggs so that anyone with an egg allergy doesn't have to miss out!

✳ Makes 12

300 g/10 oz/2 cups self-raising flour
1 tsp baking powder
85 g/3 oz/scant ½ cup caster sugar
150 g/5 oz/1 cup blueberries, plus a few extra for decoration
225 ml/8 fl oz/scant 1 cup buttermilk (or a mixture of half milk, half yogurt)
1 tsp vanilla essence
85 g/3 oz butter, melted

Preheat the oven to 200°C/400°F/Gas 6. Grease or line a 12-hole muffin pan.

Combine the flour, baking powder and sugar and sift into a large bowl, then add the blueberries.

In a separate bowl or jug, combine the buttermilk, vanilla and butter, then pour into the dry ingredients. Stir together gently until just combined, then spoon big dollops of the mixture into the prepared muffin pan. Press a few extra blueberries into the tops of the muffins so there's a generous number on the top.

Bake for about 20 minutes until risen and golden. Leave to cool in the pan for a few minutes, then transfer to a wire rack to cool.

Spiced maple and pecan munchies

Another irresistible combination that you can throw together in minutes and be munching on in less than half an hour. (And although they're pretty good cold ... you probably won't be able to leave them on the wire rack long enough to find out!)

✳ Makes 12

300 g/10 oz/2 cups self-raising flour
1 tsp baking powder
125 g/4½ oz/generous ½ cup caster sugar
½ tsp mixed spice
75 g/2¾ oz pecan nuts, roughly chopped, plus extra for sprinkling
2 eggs, beaten
75 ml/3 fl oz/scant ⅓ cup milk
100 ml/3½ fl oz/scant ½ cup plain yogurt
4 tbsp maple syrup, plus extra for brushing
85 g/3 oz butter, melted

Preheat the oven to 190°C/375°F/Gas 5. Grease or line a 12-hole muffin pan.

Combine the flour, baking powder, sugar and mixed spice and sift into a large bowl, then add the nuts.

In a separate bowl or jug, combine the eggs, milk, yogurt and syrup, then stir in the butter. Pour into the dry ingredients and stir together until just mixed. Spoon big dollops of the mixture into the prepared muffin pan and sprinkle over a few more chopped pecan nuts.

Bake for about 20 minutes until risen and golden. Leave to cool in the pan for a few minutes, then transfer to a wire rack. While still warm, brush with more maple syrup.

Lemon and almond crumbles

Lemony, almondy, moist, moreish ... what's not to like? These are another of those easy-peasy muffins that somehow elicit an air of sophistication and make you feel rather ladylike – until you find yourself trying to resist the urge to eat more than one!

✱ Makes 12

225 g/8 oz/1½ cups self-raising flour
1 tsp baking powder
150 g/5 oz/⅔ cup caster sugar
115 g/4 oz/1 cup ground almonds
1 egg, beaten
225 ml/8 fl oz/scant 1 cup milk
85 g/3 oz butter, melted
grated zest of 2 lemons
40 g/1½ oz/½ cup flaked almonds, for sprinkling
icing sugar, for dusting

Preheat the oven to 200°C/400°F/Gas 6. Grease or line a 12-hole muffin pan.

Combine the flour, baking powder and caster sugar and sift into a large bowl. Sprinkle the ground almonds into the bowl.

In a separate bowl or jug, combine the egg, milk, butter and lemon zest, then pour into the dry ingredients. Stir together until just combined, then spoon big dollops of the mixture into the prepared muffin pan. Sprinkle the tops with flaked almonds.

Bake for about 20 minutes until risen and golden. Leave to cool in the pan for a few minutes, then transfer to a wire rack to cool. Serve dusted with icing sugar.

Date and ginger honeys

Topped off with lashings of sticky honey and creamy crème fraîche, these gluten-free muffins are messy to eat, but all the better for it! Eat them while they're still warm, using a teaspoon to scoop the muffin and toppings out of the paper case. Alternatively, just serve with a lot of napkins!

✳ Makes 12

200 g/7 oz/1⅓ cup potato flour
100 g/3½ oz/⅔ cup rice flour
1 tbsp baking powder
1 tsp ground ginger
2 eggs, beaten
100 ml/3½ fl oz/scant ½ cup
    plain yogurt
75 ml/3 fl oz/scant ⅓ cup milk
5 tbsp vegetable oil
115 g/4 oz/½ cup brown sugar
100 g/3 ½ oz pitted dates,
    roughly chopped
3 pieces stem ginger in syrup,
    roughly chopped
clear honey, for drizzling
crème fraîche, for dolloping

Preheat the oven to 200°C/400°F/Gas 6. Line a 12-hole muffin pan.

Combine the flours, baking powder and ginger and sift into a large bowl.

In a separate bowl, lightly beat together the eggs, yogurt, milk, oil and sugar, then stir in the dates and about two-thirds of the stem ginger. Pour into the dry ingredients and stir together until just combined. Spoon big dollops of the mixture into the prepared muffin pan and sprinkle the remaining pieces of ginger over the top.

Bake for about 20 minutes until risen and golden. Leave to cool in the pan for a few minutes, then transfer to a wire rack to cool.

Serve slightly warm, drizzled with honey and topped with a generous dollop of crème fraîche.

Tangy rhubarb and custard

For that old-fashioned pud feel, serve these moist, tender muffins warm, topped with a big spoonful of thick, fresh custard. They'll be messy to eat, but worth getting sticky fingers for!

✳ Makes 12

300 g/10 oz/2 cups self-raising flour
1 tsp baking powder
1 tsp ground ginger
50 g/1¾ oz/4 tbsp mascarpone
125 ml/4 fl oz/½ cup milk
2 eggs, beaten
150 g/5 oz/⅔ cup soft brown sugar
115 g/4 oz butter, melted
175 g/6 oz rhubarb, chopped
ready-made custard, to serve (optional)

Preheat the oven to 200°C/400°F/Gas 6. Grease or line a 12-hole muffin pan.

Combine the flour, baking powder and ginger and sift into a large bowl.

In a separate bowl, beat the mascarpone until soft, then gradually beat in 1–2 tbsp milk until smooth and creamy, then beat in the rest with the eggs. Stir in the sugar and butter, then add the rhubarb and pour into the dry ingredients. Stir together until just combined, then spoon dollops of the mixture into the prepared muffin pan.

Bake for about 20 minutes until risen and golden. Leave to cool in the pan for a few minutes, then transfer to a wire rack to cool.

Serve on their own, or topped with a big dollop of fresh custard.

Muesli morning muffins

When you're after a dairy-free brekkie, these wholesome muffins are the way to go. Packed with oats, dried fruit and seeds, they're substantial little devils – and not too sweet – so you could almost feel like you're being healthy! (And, of course, if you're happy drinking milk, you can use regular milk in place of the soya milk.)

✳ Makes 12

250 g/9 oz/1⅔ cups self-raising flour
1 tsp baking powder
1 tsp ground ginger
100 g/3½ oz/½ cup muesli
2 tbsp pumpkin seeds
50 g/1¾ oz ready-to-eat dried apricots, chopped
2 eggs, beaten
200 ml/7 fl oz/generous ¾ cup soya milk
5 tbsp sunflower oil
50 g/1¾ oz/¼ cup soft brown sugar
5 tbsp clear honey

Preheat the oven to 200°C/400°F/Gas 6. Grease or line a 12-hole muffin pan.

Combine the flour, baking powder and ginger and sift into a large bowl.

In a separate bowl, combine the muesli and pumpkin seeds, then set aside about one-quarter of the mixture. Add the remaining muesli mixture and apricots to the flour.

In a separate bowl or jug, combine the eggs, milk, oil, sugar and honey, stirring until the honey is well mixed. Pour into the dry ingredients and stir together until just combined. Spoon big dollops of the mixture into the prepared muffin pan and sprinkle the remaining muesli mixture over the top.

Bake for about 20 minutes until risen and golden. Leave to cool in the pan for a couple of minutes, then transfer to a wire rack to cool.

Luscious lemon and raspberry

Just because you're avoiding gluten, doesn't mean you need to miss out on indulging yourself in a muffin now and again. Tender, sweet, lemony, fruity and creamy, you'll never feel deprived once you've baked a batch of these beauties! The raspberries sink to the bottom to create a dense, moist, fruity layer, topped off with a light, almondy crumb.
For something simpler, just leave out the topping and serve plain.

✳ Makes 12

100 g/3½ oz/1 cup ground
   almonds
100 g/3½oz/⅔ cup potato flour
50 g/1¾ oz/⅓ cup rice flour
150 g/5 oz/⅔ cup caster sugar
1 tbsp gluten-free baking powder
150 g/5 oz/1 cup raspberries
2 eggs, beaten
175 ml/6 fl oz/¾ cup milk
85 g/3 oz butter, melted
grated zest of 1 lemon

For the topping
150 g/5 oz mascarpone
6 tbsp gluten-free lemon curd
fresh raspberries, to decorate

Preheat the oven to 200°C/400°F/Gas 6. Line a 12-hole muffin pan with paper cases.

Combine the ground almonds, potato and rice flours, the sugar and baking powder and sift into a large bowl. (Don't worry if there are still some large bits of ground almond left in the sieve, just sprinkle them over the top.) Add the raspberries.

In a separate bowl or jug, combine the eggs, milk, butter and lemon zest, then pour into the dry ingredients and gently stir together – being careful not to break up the raspberries – until the ingredients are just mixed. Spoon big dollops of the mixture into the prepared muffin pan.

Bake for about 18 minutes until risen and golden. Leave to cool in the pan for a few minutes, then transfer to a wire rack to cool completely.

To decorate, beat together the mascarpone and lemon curd until creamy, then swirl on top of the cakes and decorate with fresh raspberries.

Peanut butter and choc chip cheekies

Kids just love these big fat muffins studded with chocolate chips and little nuggets of peanut. Throw a batch in the oven after school and they can enjoy them warm with a big glass of milk. If you want to go for a dairy-free version, use plain chocolate chips and substitute soya milk for regular milk.

✳ Makes 12

300 g/10 oz/2 cups self-raising flour
1 tsp baking powder
100 g/3 ½ oz milk chocolate chips
200 g/7 oz/generous ⅔ cup crunchy peanut butter
115 g/4 oz/ ½ cup soft brown sugar
2 eggs, beaten
200 ml/7 fl oz/generous ¾ cup milk

Preheat the oven to 200°C/400°F/Gas 6. Grease or line a 12-hole muffin pan.

Combine the flour and baking powder and sift into a large bowl, then add about three-quarters of the chocolate chips.

In a separate bowl, beat together the peanut butter and sugar, then gradually beat in the eggs and milk to make a smooth mixture. Pour into the dry ingredients and stir together until just combined, then spoon large dollops into the prepared muffin pan. Sprinkle with the remaining chocolate chips, pressing them gently into the mixture.

Bake for about 18 minutes until risen and golden. Leave to cool in the pan for a few minutes, then transfer to a wire rack to cool.

Mini fruit marvels

These cute little fruity numbers are just irresistible for mini hands and make a great tea party standard. Mix up the icing and let the kids decorate them themselves, then lay the table (or picnic rug if you're going down the teddy bear's picnic route) and have an afternoon of fun. (And if your kids don't like mixed peel, just leave it out!)

✳ Makes 24

150 g/5 oz/1 cup self-raising
   flour
½ tsp baking powder
4 tbsp caster sugar
75 ml/2½ fl oz/scant ⅓ cup milk
3 tbsp plain yogurt
1 egg, beaten
40 g/1½ oz butter, melted
grated zest of 1 orange
60 g/2 oz/6 tbsp raisins,
   plus extra to decorate
2 tbsp mixed candied peel,
   plus extra to decorate
60 g/2 oz/⅓ cup icing sugar,
   sifted
1½ –2 tsp orange juice

Preheat the oven to 190°C/375°F/Gas 5. Line two 12-hole mini muffin pans with mini muffin papers.

Combine the flour, baking powder and caster sugar and sift into a large bowl.

In a separate bowl, lightly beat together the milk, yogurt and egg to combine, then stir in the butter, orange zest and dried fruit and peel. Pour into the dry ingredients and stir until just combined, then spoon dollops of the mixture into the prepared muffin pans.

Bake for about 15 minutes until risen and golden. Leave to cool in the pans for a few minutes, then transfer to a wire rack to cool.

To decorate, mix the icing sugar and orange juice until smooth, then spoon on to the cooled muffins. Decorate each one with a raisin or a few pieces of mixed peel.

Rocky roadsters

Although the rocky road combination of nuts, marshmallows and chocolate usually goes into ice cream, there's no reason why you shouldn't throw the trio into a muffin instead. If you do, you'll find yourself with an irresistible batch of the squishiest, melty-est, chunkiest muffins you've ever seen.

✳ Makes 12

300 g/10 oz/2 cups self raising
    flour
1 tsp baking powder
3 tbsp cocoa powder
75 g/2¾ oz milk chocolate,
    chopped
60 g/2 oz/½ cup walnut pieces
60 g/2 oz mini marshmallows
    (or large marshmallows
    snipped into pieces)
150 g/5 oz/⅔ cup soft brown
    sugar
200 ml/7 fl oz/generous ¾ cup
    milk
2 eggs, beaten
75 g/2¾ oz butter, melted

Preheat the oven to 200°C/400°F/Gas 6. Grease or line a 12-hole muffin pan.

Combine the flour, baking powder and cocoa and sift into a large bowl. Reserve about one-third of the chocolate chunks and nuts, then add the rest, along with the marshmallows, to the flour.

In a separate bowl or jug, combine the sugar, milk, eggs and butter, then pour into the dry ingredients. Stir together until just combined, then spoon big dollops of the mixture into the prepared muffin pan. Gently press the reserved chocolate and nuts at random into the muffins.

Bake for about 20 minutes until risen and firm to the touch. Leave to cool in the pan for a few minutes, then transfer to a wire rack to cool.

Birthday mini muffins

Who needs a birthday cake when there are mini muffins to gobble instead? With twenty-four muffins in each batch, they're just perfect for a party – or for a very greedy birthday boy or girl!

✳ Makes 24

300 g/10 oz/2 cups self-raising flour
1 tsp baking powder
2 tbsp cocoa powder, plus extra for dusting
150 g/5 oz/⅔ cup caster sugar
100 g/3½ oz dark chocolate, chopped
1 egg, beaten
250 ml/9 fl oz/1 cup plain yogurt
2 tbsp milk
85 g/3 oz butter, melted
24 birthday candles, to decorate

Preheat the oven to 190°C/375°F/Gas 5. Grease or line a 24-hole mini muffin pan.

Combine the flour, baking powder, cocoa and caster sugar and sift into a large bowl, then add the chocolate.

In a separate bowl or jug, combine the egg, yogurt, milk and butter, then pour into the dry ingredients. Stir together until just combined, then spoon large dollops of the mixture into the prepared muffin pan, making sure there are plenty of chocolate chunks peeping through the tops of the muffins.

Bake for about 15 minutes until risen and firm to the touch. Leave to cool in the pan for a few minutes, then transfer to a wire rack to cool completely.

To serve, dust with cocoa and stick a candle in the centre of each muffin. Light and enjoy!

Figgy oatmeal muffins

Sweet, sticky and great for kids on a dairy-free diet. Although having said that, kids who do eat milk and butter will love these too, and mums and dads, and grandparents...

✳ Makes 12

50 g/1¾ oz/½ cup rolled oats
150 g/5 oz ready-to-eat dried figs, chopped
125 ml/4 fl oz/½ cup boiling water
250 g/9 oz/1⅔ cups self-raising flour
1 tsp baking powder
115 g/4 oz/½ cup caster sugar
2 eggs, beaten
150 ml/5 fl oz/scant ⅔ cup soya milk
6 tbsp sunflower oil

For the topping
75 g/2¾ oz ready-to-eat dried figs, chopped
3 tbsp clear honey
2 tsp boiling water

Preheat the oven to 200°C/400°F/Gas 6. Line a 12-hole muffin pan.

Put the oats and figs in a bowl and pour over the boiling water. Leave to soak for 10 minutes.

Combine the flour, baking powder and sugar and sift into a large bowl.

Add the eggs, milk and oil to the soaked oats and lightly beat together until combined, then pour into the dry ingredients. Stir together until just mixed, then spoon big dollops of the mixture into the prepared muffin pan.

Bake for about 20 minutes until risen and golden. Leave to cool in the pan for a few minutes, then transfer to a wire rack to cool.

While the muffins are still warm, make the topping. Put the figs, honey and water in a pan and simmer for about 1 minute. Spoon over the muffins and leave to cool.

Tropical temptations

Go exotic with these fabulously fruity muffins oozing with melting mango and tangy pineapple. Turn the heating right up, shut your eyes and imagine you're on a tropical island ... eating a muffin!

✳ Makes 12

300 g/10 oz/2 cups self-raising flour
1 tsp baking powder
150 g/5 oz/⅔ cup caster sugar
1 egg, beaten
100 ml/3½ fl oz/scant ½ cup crème fraîche
125 ml/4 fl oz/½ cup milk
grated zest of 1 lime
85 g/3 oz butter, melted
115 g/4 oz mango flesh, diced
75 g/2¾ oz pineapple, diced

Preheat the oven to 200°C/400°F/Gas 6. Grease or line a 12-hole muffin pan. Combine the flour, baking powder and sugar and sift into a large bowl.

In a separate bowl, briefly beat the egg, crème fraîche, milk and lime zest until smooth, then stir in the butter and about three-quarters of the mango and pineapple. Add to the dry ingredients and stir together until just combined. Spoon large dollops of the mixture into the prepared muffin pan, then top each muffin with the remaining mango and pineapple.

Bake for about 20 minutes until risen and golden. Leave to cool in the pan for a few minutes, then transfer to a wire rack to cool.

Espresso express

Make these in the morning when you need a bit of jet-fuel to get you going. After munching your way through the coffee-flavoured crumb specked with whole chocolate-covered coffee beans and all topped off with a lusciously creamy, sugary coffee buttercream, nothing's going to stop you!

✳ **Makes 12**

300 g/10 oz/2 cups plain flour
1 tbsp baking powder
150 g/5 oz/⅔ cup caster sugar
40 g/1½ oz/¼ cup chocolate-
    covered coffee beans
1 egg, beaten
175 ml/6 fl oz/¾ cup milk
2 tbsp Greek yogurt
2 tbsp instant coffee, dissolved in
    2 tbsp boiling water
85 g/3 oz butter, melted

For the topping
100 g/3½ oz butter, at room
    temperature
200 g/7 oz/1¾ cups icing sugar,
    sifted
2 tsp instant coffee, dissolved in
    1 tbsp boiling water
chocolate-covered coffee beans,
    to decorate

Preheat the oven to 200°C/400°F/Gas 6. Grease or line a 12-hole muffin pan.

Combine the flour, baking powder and caster sugar and sift into a large bowl, then scatter the coffee beans on top.

In a separate bowl or jug, lightly beat together the egg, milk, yogurt and coffee, then stir in the melted butter. Pour into the dry ingredients and stir together until just combined, then spoon big dollops of the mixture into the prepared muffin pan.

Bake for about 20 minutes until risen and firm to the touch. Leave to cool in the pan for a few minutes, then transfer to a wire rack to cool completely.

To decorate, beat together the butter, icing sugar and coffee until smooth and creamy. Swirl on top of the muffins and decorate with more chocolate-covered coffee beans.

Banoffee toffees

Just like the pie ... but a bit more muffiny! There's something just irresistible about the decadent combination of whipped cream, bananas and gooey, sticky, velvety toffee sauce, which makes these magical muffins the only ones to choose when you need a little bit of comfort muffin in your life.

✳ Makes 12

300 g/10 oz/2 cups plain flour
1 tbsp baking powder
1 egg, beaten
200 ml/7 fl oz/generous ¾ cup milk
150 g/5 oz/⅔ cup soft brown sugar
85 g/3 oz butter, melted
2 bananas, peeled and diced

To decorate
150 ml/5 fl oz/⅔ cup double cream
1–2 bananas, sliced
4 tbsp *dulce de leche*

Preheat the oven to 200°C/400°F/Gas 6. Grease or line a 12-hole muffin pan.

Combine the flour and baking powder and sift into a large bowl.

In a separate bowl or jug, combine the egg and milk, then stir in the sugar and melted butter. Add the banana, give it all a quick stir, then tip into the dry ingredients and stir together until just mixed. Spoon big dollops of the mixture into the prepared muffin pan.

Bake for about 20 minutes until risen and golden. Leave to cool in the pan for a few minutes, then transfer to a wire rack to cool completely.

To decorate, whip the cream until it stands in soft peaks, then spoon dollops on top of each muffin. Top with a couple of slices of banana, drizzle with *dulce de leche* and serve.

Triple choc-chunkies

This is the muffin for all you chocaholics out there. A chocolatey crumb, then big chunks of white and dark chocolate inside – and if you serve them while they're still warm, that chocolate is oh-so-gooey, and oh-so-good!

✳ Makes 12

300 g/10 oz/2 cups plain flour
1 tbsp baking powder
3 tbsp cocoa powder
150 g/5 oz/⅔ cup caster sugar
75 g/2¾ oz dark chocolate, chopped
75 g/2¾ oz white chocolate, chopped
2 eggs
125 ml/4 fl oz/½ cup soured cream
100 ml/3½ fl oz/scant ½ cup milk
85 g/3 oz butter, melted

Preheat the oven to 200°C/400°F/Gas 6. Grease or line a 12-hole muffin pan.

Combine the flour, baking powder, cocoa and sugar and sift into a large bowl. Reserve about 25 g/1 oz of the dark chocolate chunks and add the rest of the dark and white chocolate to the sifted ingredients.

In a separate bowl or jug, lightly beat together the eggs, cream and milk until smooth, then stir in the butter and pour into the dry ingredients. Stir together until just combined, then spoon large dollops of the mixture into the prepared muffin pan. Top the muffins with the reserved chunks of chocolate, pressing them gently into the mixture.

Bake for about 20 minutes until risen and firm to the touch. Leave to cool in the pan for a few minutes, then transfer to a wire rack to cool.

White chocolate, cherry and macadamia

These cheeky little numbers are just the right side of decadent indulgence. Not so naughty that you need to feel guilty, but just sweet and sticky enough to give you the feel-good hit you deserve. Slightly sharp cherries, sweet, melted white chocolate and perfectly round, nutty macadamias ... what's not to like?

✳ Makes 12

300 g/10 oz/2 cups plain flour
1 tbsp baking powder
150 g/5 oz/⅔ cup caster sugar
75 g/2¾ oz white chocolate, chopped
60 g/2 oz/½ cup dried cherries
60 g/2 oz/½ cup macadamia nuts
1 egg, beaten
100 ml/3½ fl oz/scant ½ cup soured cream
125 ml/4 fl oz/½ cup milk
85 g/3 oz butter, melted

Preheat the oven to 190°C/375°F/Gas 5. Grease or line a 12-hole muffin pan.

Combine the flour, baking powder and sugar and sift into a large bowl. Reserve about one-quarter each of the chocolate, cherries and nuts and add the rest to the flour.

In a separate bowl or jug, lightly beat the egg, soured cream and milk to combine, then stir in the butter. Pour into the dry ingredients and stir together until just combined. Spoon large dollops of the mixture into the prepared muffin pan and press the reserved chocolate, cherries and nuts into the top of each.

Bake for about 20 minutes until risen and golden. Leave to cool in the pan for a few minutes, then transfer to a wire rack to cool.

Chocolate hazelnut melts

There's something a little bit childish about these muffins filled with Nutella, which are gorgeously gooey and sticky when you bite into them – but they're too good for kids! Bake yourself a batch, put on the coffee and sit back and relax in utter decadence!

✳ Makes 12

100 g/3½ oz/scant 1 cup toasted hazelnuts, plus extra to decorate
200 g/7 oz/1⅓ cups plain flour
1 tbsp baking powder
3 tbsp cocoa powder
150 g/5 oz/⅔ cup caster sugar
1 egg, beaten
200 ml/7 fl oz/generous ¾ cup buttermilk
2 tbsp milk
85 g/3 oz butter, melted
4 tbsp Nutella or other chocolate and hazelnut spread

Preheat the oven to 190°C/375°F/Gas 5. Grease or line a 12-hole muffin pan. Put the nuts in a food processor and process until finely ground.

Combine the ground nuts with the flour, baking powder, cocoa and sugar and sift into a large bowl. (Don't worry if all the nuts don't go through, just sprinkle them over the top.)

In a separate bowl or jug, combine the egg, buttermilk and milk, then stir in the butter. Pour into the dry ingredients and stir together until just combined, then spoon small dollops of the mixture into the prepared muffin pan. Using the back of a teaspoon, make a slight indent in the mixture and spoon 1 teaspoon Nutella into the centre of each muffin. Top with the remaining mixture and press a few whole hazelnuts into the top of each one.

Bake for about 20 minutes until risen and firm to the touch. Leave to cool in the pan for a few minutes, then transfer to a wire rack to cool.

Luscious lemon and raspberry

Just because you're avoiding gluten, doesn't mean you need to miss out on indulging yourself in a muffin now and again. Tender, sweet, lemony, fruity and creamy, you'll never feel deprived once you've baked a batch of these beauties! The raspberries sink to the bottom to create a dense, moist, fruity layer, topped off with a light, almondy crumb. For something simpler, just leave out the topping and serve plain.

✳ Makes 12

100 g/3½ oz/1 cup ground
   almonds
100 g/3½ oz/⅓ cup potato flour
50 g/1¾ oz/⅓ cup rice flour
150 g/5 oz/⅔ cup caster sugar
1 tbsp gluten-free baking powder
150 g/5 oz/1 cup raspberries
2 eggs, beaten
175 ml/6 fl oz/¾ cup milk
85 g/3 oz butter, melted
grated zest of 1 lemon

For the topping
150 g/5 oz mascarpone
6 tbsp gluten-free lemon curd
fresh raspberries, to decorate

Preheat the oven to 200°C/400°F/Gas 6. Line a 12-hole muffin pan with paper cases.

Combine the ground almonds, potato and rice flours, the sugar and baking powder and sift into a large bowl. (Don't worry if there are still some large bits of ground almond left in the sieve, just sprinkle them over the top.) Add the raspberries.

In a separate bowl or jug, combine the eggs, milk, butter and lemon zest, then pour into the dry ingredients and gently stir together – being careful not to break up the raspberries – until the ingredients are just mixed. Spoon big dollops of the mixture into the prepared muffin pan.

Bake for about 18 minutes until risen and golden. Leave to cool in the pan for a few minutes, then transfer to a wire rack to cool completely.

To decorate, beat together the mascarpone and lemon curd until creamy, then swirl on top of the cakes and decorate with fresh raspberries.

Rum-raisin rumba

Light, crumbly and golden with a distinctive kick of rum, these are definitely not a breakfast muffin! Serve them plain or top with a spoonful of mascarpone or a dusting of icing sugar.

✳ Makes 12

115 g/4 oz/¾ cup raisins
3 tbsp dark rum
300 g/10 oz/2 cups self-raising flour
1 tsp baking powder
150 g/5 oz/⅔ cup caster sugar
1 egg, beaten
75 ml/3 fl oz/scant ⅓ cup milk
100 ml/3½ fl oz/scant ½ cup soured cream
85 g/3 oz butter, melted

Put the raisins and rum in a bowl and leave to soak for 1 hour.

Preheat the oven to 200°C/400°F/Gas 6. Grease or line a 12-hole muffin pan.

Combine the flour, baking powder and sugar and sift into a large bowl.

In a separate bowl or jug, lightly beat together the egg, milk and soured cream until smooth, then stir in the butter, soaked raisins and rum. Pour into the dry ingredients and stir together until just mixed, then spoon large dollops of the mixture into the prepared muffin pan.

Bake for about 20 minutes until risen and golden. Leave to cool in the pan for a few minutes, then transfer to a wire rack to cool.

Cool and creamy carrot cake

If you fancy making a dairy-free version of these muffins, just use soya milk instead of regular milk, and omit the frosting. They're still fab served plain, warm from the oven with just a drizzle of honey on top.

✳ Makes 12

300 g/10 oz/2 cups self-raising
　　flour
1 tsp baking powder
1 tsp ground cinnamon
75 g/2¾ oz/scant ¾ cup walnut
　　pieces
115 g/4 oz/½ cup soft brown
　　sugar
2 eggs, beaten
200 ml/7 fl oz/generous ¾ cup
　　milk
150 ml/5 fl oz/scant ⅔ cup
　　sunflower oil
1 large carrot, grated
finely grated zest of 1 orange

For the topping
150 g/5 oz cream cheese
50 g/1¾ oz/⅓ cup icing sugar,
　　sifted
1 tsp lemon juice
12 walnut halves

Preheat the oven to 200°C/400°F/Gas 6. Grease or line a 12-hole muffin pan.

Combine the flour, baking powder and cinnamon and sift into a large bowl, then scatter the walnut pieces on top.

In a separate bowl, combine the brown sugar, eggs, milk and oil and beat lightly until well mixed, then stir in the grated carrot and orange zest. Pour into the dry ingredients and stir together until just combined, then spoon big dollops of the mixture into the prepared muffin pan.

Bake for about 20 minutes until risen and golden. Leave to cool in the pan for a few minutes, then transfer to a wire rack to cool completely.

To decorate, beat together the cream cheese, icing sugar and lemon juice until smooth and creamy. Swirl the frosting on top of the muffins and top each one with a walnut half.

Apricot and marzipan magic

Sweet, golden, meltingly tender and so, so easy to make, these fabulous almondy, fruity muffins are just divine. You can eat them any time, but I like them mid-afternoon with a nice cup of Earl Grey in the prettiest teacup I can find.

✳ Makes 12

300 g/10 oz/2 cups plain flour
1 tbsp baking powder
100 g/3½ oz/scant ½ cup caster
  sugar
85 g/3 oz marzipan, finely grated
2 eggs, beaten
175 ml/5½ fl oz/¾ cup milk
85 g/3 oz butter, melted
85 g/3 oz ready-to-eat dried
  apricots, chopped
icing sugar, to dust (optional)

Preheat the oven to 200°C/400°F/Gas 6. Grease or line a 12-hole muffin pan.

Combine the flour, baking powder and caster sugar and sift into a large bowl, then sprinkle the grated marzipan on top.

In a separate bowl or jug, combine the eggs, milk and butter, then stir in the apricots. Pour the mixture into the dry ingredients and stir together until just combined, then spoon large dollops of the mixture into the prepared muffin pan.

Bake for about 20 minutes until risen and golden, then leave to cool in the pan for a few minutes. Transfer to a wire rack to cool.

Serve dusted with icing sugar, if you like.

Black forest muffins

If you like the gateau, you'll absolutely love the muffins! These ones don't contain liqueur like the traditional cake does, but if you fancy a boozy twist, prick the tops of the muffins and drizzle a little kirsch over each one before decorating with whipped cream and cherries.

✳ Makes 12

100 g/3½ oz plain chocolate, chopped
85 g/3 oz butter
300 g/10 oz/2 cups plain flour
1 tbsp baking powder
150 g/5 oz/⅔ cup caster sugar
2 tbsp cocoa powder
200 g/7 oz/1½ cups black cherries, halved and pitted
200 ml/7 fl oz/generous ¾ cup milk
1 egg, beaten

To decorate
150 ml/5 fl oz/scant ⅔ cup double cream
12 black cherries
dark chocolate shavings

Preheat the oven to 200°C/400°F/Gas 6. Grease or line a 12-hole muffin pan.

Put the chocolate and butter in a heatproof bowl set over a pan of simmering water and leave until melted. Stir to combine, then set aside to cool.

Combine the flour, baking powder, sugar and cocoa and sift into a large bowl, then scatter the cherries on top.

Stir the milk and egg into the cooled chocolate mixture until smooth, then pour into the dry ingredients. Stir together until just mixed, then spoon big dollops of the mixture into the prepared muffin pan.

Bake for about 20 minutes until risen and just firm to the touch. Leave to cool in the pan for a few minutes, then transfer to a wire rack to cool completely.

To decorate, whip the cream until it stands in soft peaks, then spoon dollops on top of each muffin. Top with a cherry and decorate each one with a few chocolate shavings.

Easter muffins

When you're celebrating Easter with a gluten- or dairy-intolerant muffin-eater, this is the recipe to choose. Inspired by the fruity marzipan simnel cake, these little muffins look cuter than cute topped off with baby chick yellow frosting and pastel-coloured eggs. Be sure to check the ingredients on your pastel-coloured eggs and marzipan to make sure they don't contain any dairy or gluten.

✻ Makes 12

200 g/7 oz/1⅓ cups potato flour
100 g/3½ oz/⅔ cup rice flour
1 tbsp cornflour
1 tbsp gluten-free baking powder
100 g/3½ oz/scant ½ cup caster sugar
100 g/3½ oz/⅔ cup raisins or sultanas
2 tbsp candied peel
1 egg, beaten
175 ml/6 fl oz/¾ cup soya milk
6 tbsp sunflower oil
100 g/3½ oz gluten-free marzipan, finely grated
finely grated zest of 1 lemon

To decorate
200 g/7 oz/1¾ cup icing sugar, sifted
2 tbsp lemon juice
yellow food colouring
pastel-coloured mini eggs

Preheat the oven to 200°C/400°F/Gas 6. Grease or line a 12-hole muffin pan.

Combine the flours, baking powder and caster sugar and sift into a large bowl, then add the raisins or sultanas and candied peel.

In a separate bowl or jug, combine the egg, milk and oil, then stir in the marzipan and lemon zest. Pour into the dry ingredients and stir together until just combined, then spoon large dollops of the mixture into the prepared muffin pan.

Bake for about 20 minutes until risen and golden. Leave to cool in the pan for a few minutes, then transfer to a wire rack to cool.

To decorate, mix the icing sugar and lemon juice until smooth, then add a few drops of food colouring to make a pale yellow frosting. Spoon on top of the cakes and top with mini eggs.

Spring flower favourites

Bake these creamy, lemony muffins scented with cardamom just because it's spring and the sun's shining. Or, if you're the caring, sharing type, why not whip up a batch for mum on Mother's Day?

✳ Makes 12

300 g/10 oz/2 cups plain flour
1 tbsp baking powder
150 g/5 oz/⅔ cup caster sugar
1 egg, beaten
225 ml/8 fl oz/scant 1 cup milk
grated zest of 1 lemon
seeds from 6 cardamom pods,
    crushed
85 g/3 oz butter, melted
sugar spring flowers, to decorate

For the frosting
150 g/5 oz mascarpone
3 tbsp icing sugar, sifted
1½ tsp lemon juice
yellow food colouring

Preheat the oven to 200°C/400°F/Gas 6. Grease or line a 12-hole muffin pan.

Combine the flour, baking powder and caster sugar and sift into a large bowl.

In a separate bowl or jug, combine the egg and milk, then stir in the lemon zest, cardamom seeds and butter. Pour into the dry ingredients and stir together until just combined, then spoon large dollops of the mixture into the prepared muffin pan.

Bake for 20 minutes until risen and golden. Leave to cool in the pan for a few minutes, then transfer to a wire rack to cool.

To decorate, beat together the mascarpone, icing sugar and lemon juice until smooth and creamy, then add a few drops of yellow colouring to make a pretty buttercup yellow. Swirl on top of the muffins and decorate with sugar spring flowers.

Redcurrant love hearts

With a swirled cheesecake topping on these muffins, they're hard to resist. So go on – bake up a batch for the love of your life and wow them with your baking skills! After all, how could they resist you after that...?

♥ Makes 12

300 g/10 oz/2 cups self-raising
 flour
1 tsp baking powder
150 g/5 oz/⅔ cup caster sugar
100 g/3½ oz redcurrants, plus
 extra to decorate
225 ml/8 fl oz/scant 1 cup milk
1 egg, beaten
85 g/3 oz butter, melted
1 tsp vanilla essence

For the filling
150 g/5 oz cream cheese
150 g/5 oz/⅔ cup caster sugar
1 egg, beaten
¼ tsp vanilla essence

Preheat the oven to 200°C/400°F/Gas 6. Line a 12-hole heart-shaped muffin pan with heart-shaped papers.

First make the filling. Beat together the cream cheese and sugar until creamy, then beat in the egg and vanilla until smooth and creamy. Set aside.

To make the muffins, combine the flour, baking powder and sugar and sift together into a large bowl. Strip the currants from their stems and add the fruit to the flour.

In a separate bowl or jug, combine the milk, egg, butter and vanilla, then pour over the dry ingredients. Gently stir together until just combined, then spoon big dollops of the mixture into the paper cases. Top each one with a dollop of the cream cheese mixture, swirling it into the muffin mixture.

Bake for about 20 minutes until risen and golden. Leave to cool in the pan for a few minutes, then transfer to a wire rack to cool.

To serve, top each muffin with a sprig of redcurrants.

Hallowe'en super scaries

It's the time of year to roast some squash or pumpkin and then throw it into these irresistibly sweet and spicy muffins. Look out for fake spiders and other nasties in kids' toy shops and hide a few on the plate to scare anyone else away ... leaving you with a big batch of muffins all to yourself!

✳ Makes 12

200 g/7 oz peeled, seeded butter-nut squash or pumpkin, cut into chunks
½ tbsp sunflower oil
300 g/10 oz/2 cups plain flour
1 tbsp baking powder
1 tsp ground cinnamon
1 egg, beaten
150 ml/5 fl oz/scant ⅔ cup soured cream
50 ml/1¾ fl oz milk
115 g/4 oz/½ cup soft brown sugar
60 g/2 oz butter, melted

To decorate
150 g/5 oz white chocolate
25 g/1 oz dark chocolate

Preheat the oven to 190°C/375°F/Gas 5. Put the squash in a baking dish, drizzle with the oil, then toss to coat. Roast for about 35 minutes until tender. Remove from the oven and leave to cool, then mash roughly with a fork.

To make the muffins, preheat the oven to 200°C/400°F/Gas 6. Grease or line a 12-hole muffin pan.

Combine the flour, baking powder and cinnamon and sift into a large bowl.

In a separate bowl, combine the egg, soured cream, milk, mashed squash, sugar and butter and stir together until well mixed. Pour into the dry ingredients and stir together until just combined, then spoon large dollops of the mixture into the prepared muffin pan.

Bake for about 20 minutes until risen and golden. Leave to cool in the pan for a few minutes, then transfer to a wire rack.

To decorate, melt the white chocolate in a heatproof bowl set over a pan of barely simmering water, then spoon on top of the cakes. Melt the dark chocolate in the same way in a separate bowl, then spoon into a piping bag with a very narrow nozzle. Pipe concentric circles on to each cake, then use a skewer to draw a line from the centre to the outside of each cake to make a spider's web pattern.

Fabulous fireworks

Bang! Pop! Whizz! Whether it's firework night, Bastille Day or the Fourth of July – bake up a batch of these muffin sparklers to get with the firework theme! You could go for the tasteful all-silver sparkler look, but personally I like them covered in utterly over-the-top coloured sparkling balls and stars.

✳ Makes 12

250 g/9 oz/1⅔ cup self-raising flour
1 tsp baking powder
150 g/5 oz/⅔ cup caster sugar
3 tbsp cocoa powder
4 tbsp ground almonds
2 eggs, beaten
175 ml/6 fl oz/¾ cup milk
100 g/3½ oz butter, melted

To decorate
25 g/1 oz butter
1½ tbsp cocoa powder
2 tbsp boiling water
150 g/5 oz/1⅓ cup icing sugar, sifted
tiny edible silver or coloured shiny balls and stars, for sprinkling
12 mini indoor sparklers

Preheat the oven to 200°C/400°F/Gas 6. Grease or line a 12-hole muffin pan.

Combine the flour, baking powder, sugar and cocoa and sift into a large bowl, then sprinkle the almonds into the bowl.

In a separate bowl or jug, combine the eggs, milk and butter, then pour into the dry ingredients. Stir together until combined, then spoon large dollops of the mixture into the prepared muffin pan.

Bake for about 20 minutes until risen and firm to the touch. Leave to cool in the pan for a couple of minutes, then transfer to a wire rack to cool.

To decorate, put the butter in a heatproof bowl set over a pan of simmering water and leave to melt. Stir in the cocoa until smooth, then stir in the boiling water. Gradually stir in the icing sugar and stir for about 2 minutes until glossy – if very thick, stir in a drop more water. Spoon over the muffins, then sprinkle with shiny balls and stars and stick a sparkler in the centre of each one.

Pear and cranberry muffins

Get festive and enjoy a white Christmas with these snow-topped Christmas muffins. Have everything measured out on Christmas Eve so you can whip them together and throw them in the oven in time for tearing into your stocking full of goodies the next morning!

✳ **Makes 12**

300 g/10 oz/2 cups self-raising flour
½ tsp bicarbonate of soda
150 g/5 oz/⅔ cup caster sugar
½ tsp mixed spice
2 eggs, beaten
100 ml/3½ fl oz/scant ½ cup plain yogurt
75 ml/2½ fl oz/scant ⅓ cup milk
100 g/3½ oz butter, melted
2 pears, peeled, cored and diced
60 g/2 oz/⅓ cup dried cranberries

To decorate
150 g/5 oz mascarpone
3 tbsp icing sugar, sifted
36 fresh cranberries
12 small holly leaves

Preheat the oven to 200°C/400°F/Gas 6. Grease or line a 12-hole muffin pan.

Combine the flour, bicarbonate of soda, caster sugar and mixed spice and sift into a large bowl.

In a separate bowl, combine the eggs, yogurt, milk and butter. Stir in the pears and cranberries, then pour into the dry ingredients and stir together until just combined. Spoon large dollops of the mixture into the prepared muffin pan.

Bake for about 20 minutes until risen and golden. Leave to cool in the pan for a few minutes, then transfer to a wire rack to cool.

To decorate, beat together the mascarpone and icing sugar and swirl on top of each cooled muffin, then arrange three cranberries and a holly leaf on top of each one.

Mince pie magic

Get in the festive spirit with these light and fluffy muffin mince pies – so much better than the pastry original. Break open the lightly spiced citrus crumb with a tang of Grand Marnier and find lashings of moreish mincemeat hidden inside. Serve them warm – just as they are – or for an indulgent dessert try them with brandy sauce poured over...

✳ Makes 12

300 g/10 oz/2 cups plain flour
1 tbsp baking powder
115 g/4 oz/½ cup caster sugar
½ tsp ground ginger
¼ tsp freshly grated nutmeg
175 ml/6 fl oz/¾cup milk
2 tbsp Grand Marnier
1 egg, beaten
115 g/4 oz butter, melted
finely grated zest of 1 lemon
about 6 tbsp luxury mincemeat
icing sugar and silver edible
    glitter, for dusting
holly leaves, to decorate

Preheat the oven to 200°C/400°F/Gas 6. Grease or line a 12-hole muffin pan.

Combine the flour, baking powder, caster sugar, ginger and nutmeg and sift into a large bowl.

In a separate bowl or jug, combine the milk, Grand Marnier, egg, butter and lemon zest. Pour into the dry ingredients and stir together until just combined. Half fill each muffin cup with the mixture, top with a heaped teaspoon of mincemeat, nestling it down into the mixture, then top with another dollop of muffin mixture to cover.

Bake for about 20 minutes until risen and golden. Leave to cool in the pan for a few minutes, then transfer to a wire rack to cool.

To serve, dust with icing sugar, decorate with a holly leaf and sprinkle with a little silver glitter.

cookies

Basic butter biscuit

This, to me, is the holy grail of biscuits. It's a simple, foolproof recipe that makes delicious biscuits 'au naturelle', but the beauty of it is that it can be endlessly tampered with without many ill effects.

✴ Makes 1 batch

250 g/9 oz/generous 1 cup
    butter, softened
140 g/5 oz/scant 1 cup icing
    (confectioners') sugar, sifted
1 tsp vanilla extract
1 large free-range egg yolk
375 g/13 oz/2¾ cups plain
    (all-purpose) flour, plus extra
    for dusting

Beat the butter and sugar together in a large bowl until very pale and fluffy. Add the vanilla and egg yolk and mix well. Sift in the flour and mix until it forms a firm dough. You may need to get your hands in here and work it into a smooth ball. Wrap the dough in cling film and plonk it in the refrigerator for an hour. You can freeze it at this stage very happily if you wish.

Preheat the oven to 190°C/375°F/Gas Mark 5 and line 2 baking sheets with a silicone liner.

Roll out the dough on a lightly floured surface until it is about 3 mm/⅛ inch thick, then cut out the shapes you require and place on your lined baking sheets. Bake for 10–12 minutes or until the biscuits are pale golden. Transfer the biscuits to a wire rack where they will harden as they cool. Yum.

Basic shortbread

Another humdinger, this shortbread is a treat by itself, but is also the basis for endless variations on a theme. It is very easy to make and utterly delicious. Perfectomondo.

✳ Makes 1 batch

250 g/9 oz/generous 1 cup
  butter, softened, plus extra
  for greasing (if needed)
50 g/2 oz/¼ cup caster
  (superfine) sugar
250 g/9 oz/1¾ cups plain
  (all-purpose) flour
125 g/4½ oz/1 cup cornflour
  (cornstarch)

Preheat the oven to 170°C/325°F/Gas Mark 3.

Cream the butter and sugar together in a large bowl until pale and fluffy. Sift the flour and cornflour on to the butter mixture and mix until you have a lovely smooth dough. At this stage you can either press it into a square tin, which you have lightly greased, and bake straight away or form it into a fat sausage and wrap it in cling film. Make the sausage as fat as you want the biscuits to be round and chill the dough in the refrigerator for at least an hour.

Unwrap the dough and slice into rounds about 1.5 cm/ ⅝ inch thick. Place the rounds on a silicone-lined baking tray and bake for about 30–40 minutes until pale and golden. Transfer the shortbread to a wire tray to cool.

If you are using a tin, cut the shortbread in the tin while it is still warm and leave to cool in the tin.

Rich Tea

I think of Rich Tea biscuits as the ultimate in functional everyday biscuits – slightly frugal and, if I'm honest, not that enjoyable, but something to dunk into a cup of tea. It's a puritanical biscuit – it will not lead you into wickedness. I think this version might possibly make you consider toying with wickedness, if not actually going the whole hog. They are plain, but like all those secretaries in *James Bond* films, when they whip off their glasses, 'why – Miss Jones, you are beautiful...' Just one word of warning: they really, really do need to be made with unsalted butter. Sorry.

✳ Makes 1 batch

225 g/8 oz/1⅔ cups plain (all-purpose) flour, plus extra for dusting
1 tbsp baking powder (yes, really)
75 g/3 oz/scant ½ cup caster (superfine) sugar
¼ tsp salt
175 g/6 oz/¾ cup unsalted butter, cubed
A little milk

Preheat the oven to 190°C/375°F/Gas Mark 5 and line 2 baking sheets with silicone liners.

Place all the dry ingredients in a large bowl, then add the butter and rub it in with your fingertips until you have a consistency of fine breadcrumbs. Add enough milk, a dessertspoon at a time, until you have a firm dough (generally, I use 2–3 spoons). You don't need to chill the dough, but it keeps well in the refrigerator for about 3 days if you want to make it in advance.

Roll out the dough on a lightly floured surface as thin as you can, about 2 mm/1⁄16 inch would be good if possible. Cut out circle shapes and place them on your lined baking sheets. Prod them all over with a fork and bake for 8–10 minutes until golden. Transfer the biscuits to a wire rack to cool.

Digestives

I did wonder whether it was a bit risky putting in a recipe for the digestive, which has to be one of the most recognizable and un-mucked-about biscuits in the UK. If you are reading this outside the UK, you'll have to believe me – they are an institution. All I'll say is, no, they are not identical to those ones in the red packet, but they do contain the 'essence of digestive'. By jiminy they are good: easy, economical and comforting. All the things a digestive should be.

✷ **Makes 1 batch**

100 g/4 oz/⅔ cup wholemeal (whole-wheat) flour
40 g/1½ oz/¼ cup plain white (all-purpose) flour, plus extra for dusting
½ tsp baking powder
1 tbsp oats
120 g/4½ oz/9 tbsp butter, softened
100 g/4 oz/½ cup soft light brown sugar
4 tbsp milk

Preheat the oven to 190°C/375°F/Gas Mark 5 and line 2 baking sheets with silicone liners.

Mix the flours, baking powder and oats together in a large bowl. In another bowl, cream the butter and sugar together and add the flour mix to this. Stir in the milk, a little at a time, until you have a thick dough.

Knead the dough on a floured surface until it's lovely and smooth (albeit speckled slightly with the oats), then roll out to about 3 mm/⅛ inch thick and cut into rounds. Plonk them on your lined baking sheets, prick all over with a fork and bake for about 15 minutes until golden.

Transfer the biscuits to a wire rack to cool, then store them in an airtight tin. Put the kettle on...

Ginger biscuits

You can't have a biscuit book without ginger biscuits. It would be wrong. These are the unsophisticated, gorgeously moreish ones that positively reek of ground ginger and which are very popular with both children and adults. A biscuit with no drawbacks as far as I
am concerned.

✳ Makes 1 batch

150 g/5 oz/generous 1 cup
    self-raising (self-rising) flour
½ tsp bicarbonate of soda
    (baking soda)
2 tsp ground ginger
1 tsp ground cinnamon
2 tsp caster (superfine) sugar
50 g/2 oz/4 tbsp butter
2 tbsp golden (corn) syrup

Preheat the oven to 190°C/375°F/Gas Mark 5 and line 2 baking sheets with silicone liners.

Sift together all the dry ingredients in a large bowl. Heat the butter and golden syrup gently in a pan and when the butter has melted, pour it over the dry ingredients. Mix well until you have a soft dough. If it's a bit sticky, sprinkle a little more flour on to it until you get a consistency you can comfortably handle.

Using your hands, form small balls of the mixture, flatten them slightly and place them on your lined baking sheets, allowing a little space between them as they spread. Bake for about 15 minutes until golden and gorgeous-looking.

Let the biscuits cool and harden on the baking sheets for a bit before lifting them on to wire racks to cool completely.

Anzac biscuits

An old colleague of mine, Ros, introduced me to Anzac biscuits. I was completely smitten with them – chewy, oaty, coconutty and just plain old yummy. Luckily for me she gave me the recipe. I understand that they were originally made by the women of the Australian and New Zealand Army Corps (ANZAC) for the men during World War 1. Another little interesting fact: they are never to be known as 'cookies', but must always be referred to as 'biscuits'. It's the law. Look online if you don't believe me!

✳ Makes 1 batch

100 g/4 oz/1⅓ cups rolled oats
150 g/5 oz/generous 1 cup plain (all-purpose) flour
100 g/4 oz/½ cup soft light brown sugar
50 g/2 oz/scant ½ cup desiccated (dry unsweetened) coconut
115 g/4 oz/8 tbsp butter
2 tbsp golden (corn) syrup
1 tbsp hot water
½ tsp bicarbonate of soda (baking soda)

Preheat the oven to 190°C/375°F/Gas Mark 5 and line 2 baking sheets with silicone liners.

Mix the oats, flour, sugar and coconut together in a large bowl. Heat the butter and golden syrup gently in a pan until the butter has melted.

In another bowl, mix the hot water and bicarbonate of soda together and add the mixture to the pan of butter and golden syrup. Watch out for froth-central, then tip the whole lot on top of the oat mixture and stir away. Plop dessertspoonfuls of the mixture on to your lined baking sheets, allowing a little space between them as they spread, and flatten slightly. Bake for about 10 minutes until golden.

Let the biscuits cool and set on the baking sheets for a few minutes before lifting them onto wire racks to cool completely.

Custard creams

I *really* love Custard Creams. So it was always going to be a bit of a struggle to find a recipe that did them justice. I have experimented, trialled, jiggled and wiggled, and I have to say that this one is good. It is an adaptation of a recipe by she-who-must-be-obeyed, Nigella Lawson.

✳ Makes 1 batch

175 g/6 oz/1¼ cups plain (all-purpose) flour, plus extra for dusting
3 tbsp custard powder (not the sachets you add hot water to – proper custard powder)
1 tsp baking powder
60 g/2½ oz/4½ tbsp unsalted butter
60 g/2½ oz/4½ tbsp white vegetable fat
3 tbsp icing (confectioners') sugar
1 large free-range egg
1 tbsp milk

Filling:
50 g/2 oz/4 tbsp unsalted butter, softened
1 tbsp custard powder
100 g/4 oz/1 cup icing (confectioners') sugar, sifted
Few drops of hot water (optional)

Preheat the oven to 190°C/350°F/Gas Mark 5 and line 2 baking sheets with silicone liners.

Pop the flour, custard powder and baking powder into a large bowl. Cut the butter and white fat into little pieces and rub them into the dry ingredients until you have the consistency of sand. Add the sugar and mix until it is well combined.

In another bowl, beat the eggs lightly with the milk and pour on to the flour mixture, then mix it well (go on, get yer hands in there) and form it into a ball. Wrap the dough in cling film and leave to chill in the refrigerator for at least 30 minutes. You can freeze it at this stage too – handy.

Roll out the dough on a lightly floured surface until it is about 3 mm/⅛ inch thick. Cut the sheet of dough into long strips about 3 cm/1¼ inches wide and then cut the strips into 4 cm/1½ inch lengths. Lay the little biscuits on your lined baking sheets and bake for about 15 minutes.

Transfer the biscuits to a wire rack to cool while you make the filling. Cream the butter, custard powder and sugar together in a large bowl until light and fluffy. If the mixture seems a little stiff, add a few drops of hot water and beat it in until it is the consistency you are after. Sandwich 2 biscuits together with the creamy, custardy filling and enjoy.

Lemon biscuits (mark one)

This is another easy peasy classic biscuit, which is just lemony enough to brighten up a dull day.

✻ Makes 1 batch

1 batch Basic Butter Biscuit dough (see p.190), but omit the vanilla extract
Finely grated zest and juice of 1 large unwaxed lemon
Plain (all-purpose) flour, for dusting
50 g/2 oz/½ cup icing (confectioners') sugar, sifted

Make up the biscuit dough according to the instructions on page 190 and add the lemon zest. Knead it in well until it is evenly distributed. Cover the dough and leave to chill in the refrigerator for about an hour.

Preheat the oven to 190°C/375°F/Gas Mark 5 and line a baking sheet with a silicone liner.

Roll the dough out on a lightly floured surface to a thickness of about 3 mm/⅛ inch and cut out circle shapes. They don't have to be circles, they can be elephant shapes if you want, but I always make circular lemon biscuits. I don't know why. I just do. Place them on your lined baking sheet and bake for 10–12 minutes or until the biscuits are pale golden.

Transfer to a wire rack to cool. Once they are cold, make up a simple and quite runny lemon icing with the sugar and lemon juice. Since lemons don't come with a message stating how much juice they contain, may I suggest that you thin the icing with a few drops of hot water or thicken it with a smidgen more icing sugar until it is the consistency of single cream. Drizzle the icing randomly over the biscuits and leave to dry and harden before putting in an airtight tin (or in your mouth).

Lemon biscuits (mark two)

I think lemon and almond go particularly well together. These are really easy to make and as an added extra, don't even need rolling out. They are also very versatile. If you don't want lemony ones (how odd), omit the zest and add whatever jam takes your fancy.

✳ Makes 1 batch

110 g/4 oz/½ cup caster (superfine) sugar
220 g/7½ oz/scant 1 cup butter, softened
60 g/2½ oz/⅔ cup icing (confectioners') sugar
1 large free-range egg yolk
150 g/5 oz/1⅔ cups ground almonds
1 tsp almond extract
Finely grated zest and juice of 1 large unwaxed lemon
300 g/10 oz/1½ cups plain (all-purpose) flour
1 tsp baking powder
1 x small jar of lemon curd (you'll need about 120 g/4½ oz or so)

Preheat the oven to 190°C/375°F/Gas Mark 5 and line 2 baking sheets with silicone liners.

Beat the caster sugar and butter together in a large bowl until very pale and fluffy. Beat in the icing sugar, egg yolk, ground almonds, almond extract, zest and 2 teaspoons of the lemon juice. Give it a good thrashing. Sift in the flour and baking powder and stir until everything is combined.

Form a blob of the mixture into a ball just a bit smaller than a golf ball and place on your lined baking sheets. Keep going, leaving a space between all your golf balls. With your thumb, squish down to form a little well in the now flattened ball and fill with a little dollop of lemon curd (not too much or it will overflow and burn). Bake for about 10–12 minutes until the biscuits are golden and gorgeous.

Transfer to a wire rack to cool.

WARNING: don't be greedy and eat them while warm – the lemon curd will still be molten hot.

Lemon puffs

These biscuits in their traditional, shop-bought form seem to be in the league of 'love them or loathe them'. This version is less challenging and an absolute cinch to make. I would say though, that unlike most of the biscuits in this book, they do need eating on the day you make them.

Preheat the oven to 200°C/400°F/Gas Mark 6 and line 2 baking sheets with silicone liners.

Place the pastry on a lightly floured surface and give it a couple of extra rolls in both directions – you just want to thin it out a tiny bit more. Cut the pastry into strips about 3 mm/⅛ inches wide and then cut those strips into 3 mm/⅛ inch squares. Prod them several times with a fork and place them on your lined baking sheets.

In a little bowl, break up the egg white with a fork, then add the caster sugar and lemon juice and whisk with a fork just enough to amalgamate it. You don't want to add air to the egg white. Using a pastry brush, carefully brush a little of the mixture over the top of each pastry square. Try not to spill too much mixture over the edge of the pastry as it will burn on the tray. Sprinkle each square with a little more caster sugar and bake for about 10 minutes until they are puffy and golden. Keep an eye on them because once burnt they are horrid. Transfer the biscuits to a wire rack to cool.

To make the filling, cream the butter and icing sugar together in a large bowl until light and fluffy, then beat in the lemon zest. If the mixture is a bit thick, add the lemon juice slowly until you have a spreadable consistency. Once the pastry squares are cool, sandwich 2 together with the lemon butter cream.

✻ Makes 1 batch

375 g/13 oz packet ready-rolled puff pastry
Plain (all-purpose) flour, for dusting
1 large free-range egg white
2 tsp caster (superfine) sugar, plus extra for sprinkling
Juice of ½ lemon

Filling:
50 g/2 oz/4 tbsp butter, softened
100 g/4 oz/½ cup icing (confectioners') sugar, sifted
Grated zest of 1 unwaxed lemon
Juice of ½ lemon (optional)

Macaroons Vegas style

Now, there seem to be as many ways to make these little beauties as there are days in the week. I've plumped for the one which uses minimum ingredients and has maximum deliciousness. I do have a tendency to slither towards my pots of colours and tint all sorts of food inappropriately. I'm sorry, I can't help it. There is an argument for having coloured coconut macaroons in the children's section of the book, but as the colour is entirely optional, it's here instead. If you do use colours, use a tiny, tiny drop of liquid food colouring, or a dab of food colouring paste, which you can buy in sugar craft shops. Go for colour, I say.

✴ Makes 1 batch

175 g/6 oz/1¼ cups desiccated
   (dry unsweetened) coconut
4 large free-range egg whites
110 g/4 oz/½ cup caster
   (superfine) sugar
Tiny pinch of salt
Food colouring (optional)

Preheat the oven to 190°C/375°F/Gas Mark 5 and line 2 baking sheets with silicone liners.

Place everything except the food colouring (if using) in a large heatproof bowl and give it a good stir, then place the bowl over a pan of barely simmering water. Do not let the base of the bowl touch the water. Stir constantly (can be quite gentle – nothing too arduous) for 5–6 minutes until the mixture suddenly changes consistency and goes really thick and gooey – you'll know when you get there, believe me.

If you are going for the natural look, place spoonfuls of the mixture (as big as you want the macaroons to be as they do not spread very much) on to your lined baking sheets, then flatten them slightly and pop them in the oven. If you want coloured ones, divide the mixture into as many bowls as you want colours and tint away, before spooning blobs on to your baking sheets. Bake for about 15 minutes until golden, then leave to cool on a wire rack.

Nutty noodles

When I was a child I remember doing a lot of baking and once made some peanut butter biscuits. I was very excited by the recipe and thought they sounded delicious. They were possibly the most revolting thing ever to have been created in our kitchen and scarred me psychologically, they were so bad. It was with some trepidation I started experimenting again with peanut butter biscuits. I am so glad I did. Not only have my scars healed without the expense of a private counsellor, but I am now officially keen on peanut butter biscuits.

✱ Makes 1 batch

110 g/4 oz/8 tbsp butter, softened
110 g/4 oz/8 tbsp soft light brown
   sugar
50 g/2 oz crunchy peanut butter
1 large free-range egg
275 g/10 oz/2 cups plain
   (all-purpose) flour
100 g/4 oz/⅔ cup honey-roasted
   peanuts, roughly chopped

Preheat the oven to 190°C/375°F/ Gas Mark 5 and line 2 baking sheets with silicone liners.

Cream the butter and sugar together in a large bowl until pale and fluffy, then beat in the peanut butter and egg. Stir in the flour and add the chopped peanuts.

Grab a small ball of the dough (as big as you want your biscuits), roll it into a ball and flatten it with your fingers until it is about 5 mm/¼ inch thick then place on your lined sheet. Keep going until you have used up all the dough. Bake for 10–15 minutes until golden then leave the biscuits to cool on a wire rack.

Bourbons

These biscuits are yet another classic. All I'd ask is that you use a really good quality cocoa powder. It makes all the difference. This dough is a dream to handle and the resulting biscuits are far more chocolatey than the shop-bought ones. Lovely.

✳ Makes 1 batch

50 g/2 oz/4 tbsp butter, softened
50 g/2 oz/¼ cup caster (superfine) sugar
1 tbsp golden (corn) syrup
110 g/4 oz/¾ cup plain (all-purpose) flour, plus extra for dusting
½ tsp bicarbonate of soda (baking soda)
15 g/½ oz cocoa powder

Filling:
50 g/2 oz/4 tbsp butter, softened
100 g/4 oz/1 cup icing (confectioners') sugar, sifted
2 tsp cocoa powder
Few drops of hot water (optional)

Preheat the oven to 190°C/375°F/Gas Mark 5 and line 2 baking sheets with silicone liners.

Cream the butter and sugar together in a large bowl until it is pale and fluffy, then beat in the golden syrup. Sift in the flour, bicarbonate of soda and cocoa, and mix until you have a stiff dough.

Knead the dough well, then roll the dough out on a floured surface to a depth of about 4 mm/¼ inch. Cut the dough into long strips about 2.5 cm/1 inch wide, then cut these strips into 5 cm/2 inch lengths. Transfer them to your lined baking trays and prod them several times with a fork. Bake for about 15 minutes until darkened slightly and smelling all chocolatey. What you want to watch out for is slight scorching around the edges. Whip them out of the oven if you see this.

Transfer the biscuits to a wire rack to cool while you make the filling. Cream the butter, icing sugar and cocoa together in a large bowl, adding a few drops of hot water if you need to, until you have a good, spreadable consistency.

When the biscuits are cold, sandwich 2 biscuits together and leave for at least an hour before eating so that the filling can firm up.

Oo-oo biscuits

Right, they are called oo-oo biscuits because people say 'oo' when they see them and then 'ooooooo' when they taste them. And calling them cinnamon-nut-crispy-biscuits seemed too dull. They are in the everyday section because, although impressive-looking, they are very easy.

❋ Makes 1 batch

110 g/4 oz/½ cup caster (superfine) sugar
275 g/10 oz/2 cups plain (all-purpose) flour, plus extra for dusting
110 g/4 oz/8 tbsp white vegetable fat
About 2 tbsp water
3 tbsp butter, softened
2 tbsp caster (superfine) sugar, plus extra for sprinkling
1 tsp ground cinnamon
4 tbsp finely chopped nuts

Preheat the oven to 190°C/375°F/Gas Mark 5 and line 2 baking sheets with silicone liners.

Place the sugar and flour in a large bowl, add the white vegetable fat and rub it in with your fingertips until you have a fairly chunky mix, with some pieces of fat about pea size remaining. Add enough water a little bit at a time until a dough forms.

Knead the dough briefly then roll it out on a lightly floured surface to a rectangle of about 40 x 26 cm/16 x 10½ inches (don't go getting too strict here). Spread the soft butter all over the dough, then mix the sugar and cinnamon in a bowl and scatter that evenly all over. Scatter the nuts over the sugar cinnamon mix, then, beginning at the long side, start to roll the dough up tightly. Seal the end of the dough with a little water dabbed over the long edge and cut the roll into 5 mm/¼ inch slices. Place the slices on your lined baking trays, leaving space between them as they spread during cooking. Sprinkle with sugar and bake for 10–12 minutes until golden brown.

Transfer the slices to a wire rack to cool. The hardest bit is leaving them until they are cold. They crisp up as they cool, so you do need to go and water the garden so you aren't tempted by the warm, buttery cinnamony smell that calls you...

Jammy splodgers

What can I say about these classic biscuits? They are brilliant and taste good, look fantastic and always get the 'oooh, oooh, oooh' response required when one has made something.

✳ Makes 1 batch

1 batch Basic Butter Biscuit dough (see p.190)
Plain (all-purpose) flour, for dusting
Jam (any flavour)
Glacé Icing (see p.17), optional
Sprinkles (optional)

✳ Also pictured, with sprinkles, on p.212.

Make up the dough and chill according to the instructions on page 190.

Preheat the oven to 190°C/375°F/Gas Mark 5 and line 2 baking sheets with silicone liners.

Roll out the dough on a lightly floured surface until it is about 5 mm/¼ inch thick. You will need 2 circular cutters, one smaller than the other. Using the large cutter, cut out an even number of large circles, then remove the centre of half the circles with the smaller cutter. Place all the biscuits on your lined baking sheets and bake for 10-12 minutes until pale golden, then leave them to cool on wire racks.

When the biscuits are cold, take one of the solid rings and spread a thin layer of jam over it, then take a biscuit with a hole and plop it on top. *Voilà.* You could leave it here, but to really fly the flag for these delicacies, why not spread a thin layer of glacé icing over the top and then smother in sprinkles?

Iced rings

These biscuits are surely a childhood staple? Crispy, colourful and you can slide them onto your fingers, these are known as 'Charlie and Lola Biscuits' in our house. Anyone familiar with the truly wonderful *Charlie and Lola* by Lauren Child will understand why. You can buy gel food colours online from sugar-craft suppliers.

✻ Makes 1 batch

1 batch Basic Butter Biscuit
    dough (see p.190)
Plain (all-purpose) flour,
    for dusting
1 batch Glacé Icing (see p.17)
Gel food colours

✻ Pictured here with Jammy
    Splodgers (see p.210).

Preheat the oven to 190°C/375°F/Gas Mark 5 and line a baking sheet with a silicone liner.

Make up the dough and chill according to the instructions on page 190.

Roll out the dough on a lightly floured surface to about 5 mm/¼ inch thick. You will need 2 round cutters, one bigger than the other. Using the large cutter, cut out rounds, then cut smaller rounds out of all the biscuits – you can roll up the inside circles and use them again to make more biscuits.

Place the rounds on your lined baking sheet and bake for about 10 minutes until pale golden. Transfer the biscuits to a wire rack to cool completely.

Make the Glacé Icing according to the instructions on page 17 then split the icing into 3 of 4 small bowls and tint them different colours using the gels. Spread a thin layer of icing over a biscuit, then with a teaspoon of contrasting coloured icing, wave it across the top of the iced biscuit in a zigzag manner. The first layer of icing must still be wet at this stage. Quickly grab your cocktail stick and drag it through the stripes you have just made. Look and marvel at your wonderful creation. Leave to dry before showing off.

Niced gems

Hands up those who didn't have these at childhood parties?
My problem with the original is that they promised a lot but delivered
little. The biscuit base was always a bit yucky and dry and the icing
hurt your mouth. They are aesthetically hard to beat though, and this
is my version. They are bigger – and I think taste better.

✳ Makes 1 batch

1 batch Basic Butter Biscuit
    dough (see p.190)
Plain (all-purpose) flour,
    for dusting
1 batch Royal Icing (see p.17)
Gel colours

Preheat the oven to 190°C/375°F/Gas Mark 5 and line a
baking sheet with a silicone liner.

Make up dough and chill according to instructions on
page 190.

Roll out the dough on a floured surface until it is 5 mm/
¼ inch thick and cut out rounds with a small cutter. Place
the rounds on your lined baking sheet and bake for about
10 minutes until pale and golden. Transfer the biscuits to a
wire rack to cool.

Meanwhile, make the Royal Icing according to the instructions
on page 17 then divide into however many bowls you want
colours. Tint the icing with the gel colours and mix well.

You will need several parchment-paper piping bags and
several star-shaped nozzles (or you could get away with one
and keep washing it up).

When the biscuits are cold, place a star nozzle in the end
of your parchment-paper piping bag and half fill with the
icing. Fold over the top of the bag and splodge or swirl on the
biscuits. There doesn't need to be any fancy technique here.
A straight plop or a minor swirl will look lovely. Leave to dry
for at least 4 hours.

Gingerbread gangland

How can you possibly have a biscuit book without gingerbread men? This dough is very easy to make and you don't end up with those hard-as-stone biscuits. I implore you to go to town with the decoration. There is room for some minor acts of subversion here – I like to turn the gingerbread boys and girls into really naughty people, sticking their tongues out and forgetting to put their trousers on. Shun the world of currant buttons, embrace the icing bag and take the road to gingerbread badness...

✳ Makes 1 batch

350 g/12 oz/2½ cups plain (all-purpose) flour (but you may need more)
1 tsp bicarbonate of soda (baking soda)
2 tsp ground ginger
100 g/4 oz/8 tbsp butter
175 g/6 oz/scant 1 cup soft light brown sugar
1 large free-range egg
4 tbsp golden (corn) syrup
4 tbsp Royal Icing (see p.17)
Food colouring gels
Silver dragées

Sift the flour, bicarbonate of soda and ginger into a large bowl. Add the butter and rub it in with your fingertips until you have a mixture resembling fine breadcrumbs. Add the sugar and give it a good mix.

In another bowl, beat the egg and golden syrup together. I find a whisk works wonders here. Tip it over the flour mix and stir well. You may find it easier to get your hands in at this point. Sometimes the dough can be a bit on the sticky side. Keep sprinkling over flour and working it in until you have a lovely smooth dough.

Wrap the dough in cling film and leave to chill in the fridge for at least 30 minutes, but an hour would be better.

Preheat the oven to 190°C/375°F/Gas Mark 5 and line 2 baking sheets with silicone liners.

Roll the dough out on a lightly floured surface to a thickness of about 4 mm/¼ inch. Cut out the required shapes, place them slightly apart on your lined baking sheets and bake for

12–15 minutes until golden. Leave to cool slightly on the baking sheets before transferring them to a wire rack to cool completely.

When the biscuits are cold, make the icing according to the instructions on page 17. You will need several parchment-paper piping bags and size 2 nozzles. Divide the icing into as many colours as you want and tint with the gels. Place a blob of icing in each piping bag and pipe away to your heart's content. I like to pipe 2 dots for eyes and place the silver dragées on top. Leave them to dry before showing them to people and laughing loudly.

Glitter bics

As you can see from the photo, so great was the glittering stardom of these biscuits that the paparazzi turned up...

★ Makes 1 batch

1 batch Basic Butter Biscuit dough (see p.190)
Plain (all-purpose) flour, for dusting
1 batch Glacé Icing (see p.17)
Edible glitter

Make up the dough according to the instructions on page 190, then cover and leave to chill for at least 30 minutes.

Preheat the oven to 190°C/375°F/Gas Mark 5 and line 2 baking sheets with silicone liners.

Roll the dough out on a lightly floured surface to between 3–4 mm/⅛ inch thick and cut out whatever shapes you like. Place the shapes on your lined baking sheets and bake for about 10 minutes until pale golden. Transfer the biscuits to a wire rack to cool while you make the icing.

Make the icing quite thin according to the instructions on page 17, as it is to act as a glue for the glitter as much as anything. When the biscuits are cool, spread some glitter out on a large flat plate. Brush or spread the icing over the entire top surface of the biscuit and then immediately place the biscuit, icing side down, on to the glitter. Give it a gentle wiggle to make sure the entire surface has been covered in glitter, then pick the little devil up and pop it back on the wire rack to set.

Note to parents: edible glitter is poorly absorbed by the body. What goes in, must come out. Do not be alarmed...

Hearts

I think messages piped on to food items are simply splendid. I make a lot of cakes and once I made my husband a huge heart-shaped biscuit with the message, 'Look ... it's not a cake!' Any message would work. Without the messaging service, these make particularly lovely girlie biscuits. May I suggest making a hole in the top of the biscuit before it goes into the oven? They can then be threaded with ribbon and hung up in a beautiful and pleasing manner. I thank you.

♥ Makes 1 batch

1 batch Basic Butter Biscuit
   dough (see p.190)
Plain (all-purpose) flour,
   for dusting
1 batch Glacé Icing (see p.17)
   tinted red or pink
1 tbsp Royal Icing (see p.17)
Gold dragées (optional)

Make up the dough according to the instructions on page 190, then cover and leave to chill for at least 30 minutes.

Preheat the oven to 190°C/375°F/Gas Mark 5 and line a baking sheet with a silicone liner.

Roll out the dough on a lightly floured surface to about 5 mm/¼ inch thick and cut out heart shapes with a heart-shaped cutter. If you are going to hang up the biscuits, use a skewer to prod a hole in the top of the biscuits before you bake them. Place the biscuits on your lined baking sheet and bake for 10 minutes until pale golden. Transfer the biscuits to a wire rack to cool.

When the biscuits are cold, make the Glacé Icing according to the instructions on page 17 and colour the icing red or pink, or whatever colours you choose. Ice the biscuits using a small palette knife and leave to dry on a wire rack for about an hour.

Make the Royal Icing according to the instructions on page 17 then place it in a piping bag with a size 2 nozzle (optional) and pipe away – messages, dots, swirls – whatever you like. Add gold dragées at will. Leave the icing to harden for about 2 hours before presenting your work.

Chocolate fingers

I have never met a person who doesn't like these biscuits, really, never. These biscuits are extremely easy to make, you don't need any equipment and there are plenty of finger-licking opportunities. You can also make them as huge or as tiny as you like. Perfect.

✳ Makes 1 batch

1 batch Basic Butter Biscuit
    dough (see p.190)
300 g/10 oz milk, dark or
    white chocolate

Make up the dough according to the instructions on page 190, cover with cling film and leave to chill for at least 30 minutes.

Preheat the oven to 190°C/375°F/Gas Mark 5 and line 2 baking sheets with silicone liners.

Pull off gobstopper-sized pieces (or larger if you want giant's fingers) from the dough and roll into long, thin sausage shapes. They will spread a bit, so you may want to make them thinner than you want your finished biscuit to be. Arrange all your fingers (dough ones, not your fingers) on your lined baking sheets and bake for about 10 minutes or until pale golden. Leave the fingers to cool on the baking sheets.

Melt whichever chocolate you are using in a heatproof bowl set over a pan of barely simmering water, but don't let the base of the bowl touch the water. Drizzle the chocolate over a cooled biscuit. I do this over the bowl, so the drips go back into the molten chocolate. Lay the finger back on to the silicone-lined tray and get on with the next one....

You might find that having melted chocolate all over your fingers is more than you can bear and may need to stop to lick them once or twice. Depending on your thoughts about kitchen hygiene, you may wish to wash your hands after slobbering all over the place – your choice.

Alfajores

I feel very honoured to have been allowed to add this recipe to the book. The very wonderful Cecilia, a great Argentinian baker, very kindly gave me the recipe. These biscuits are extremely moreish. You can just buy *dulce de leche* in a jar and spoon it out if you don't have time to make it.

✳ Makes 1 batch

300 g/10 oz/1¼ cups butter
100 g/4 oz/½ cup caster (superfine) sugar
4 large free-range egg yolks
½ tsp vanilla extract
300 g/10 oz/scant 2¼ cups plain (all-purpose) flour, plus extra for dusting
2 tsp baking powder
Pinch of salt
1 x 397 g/14 oz can condensed milk

Cream the butter and sugar together in a large bowl until light and fluffy. Add the egg yolks and vanilla and beat away. Add all the dry ingredients and form the mixture into a ball. Wrap the dough in cling film and leave to chill in the refrigerator for at least 30 minutes.

Preheat the oven to 190°C/375°F/Gas Mark 5 and line 2 baking sheets with silicone liners. Roll out the dough on a lightly floured surface until it is about 3 mm/⅛ inch thick and cut out rounds. Place the rounds on your lined baking trays and bake for about 15 minutes. Transfer the biscuits to a wire rack to cool.

To make the *dulce de leche*, either place the unopened can of condensed milk in a saucepan of boiling water and leave to simmer for 3 hours – don't let the pan run dry. Leave the can to cool, then open it and *voilà*! Caramel gorgeousness. Alternatively, place the milk in a large microwaveable bowl and set the microwave on a medium setting and cook for a minute. Every minute you need to stop and stir. Really. Don't walk away. The great thing, though, is that in 5 or 6 minutes you've got caramel. You'll know it's ready when it's golden brown and thickened up a bit. Leave to cool.

When the caramel has cooled, sandwich 2 biscuits together with it. The biscuits are really crumbly and break easily. If the caramel is too hard to spread, give it 10 seconds (no more) in the microwave to soften it up slightly.

Sophisticated chocolate sandwiches

Still using the basic biscuit recipe here, but the addition of a dark chocolate ganache and some icing sugar, and the sneaky use of a fork, transports these biscuits to a world away from a Bourbon.

✳ Makes 1 batch

1 batch Basic Butter Biscuit
    dough (see p.190)
100 g/4 oz dark chocolate
    (at least 70% cocoa solids)
100 ml/3½ fl oz/generous
    ⅓ cup double (heavy) cream
1 tbsp icing (confectioners')
    sugar, for dusting

Preheat the oven to 190°C/375°F/Gas Mark 5 and line 2 baking sheets with silicone liners.

Make up the dough according to the instructions on page 190. You do not need to chill the dough for this recipe.

Take gobstopper-sized pieces of dough, about 2.5 cm/1 inch across, and form them into balls. Place a ball on your lined baking sheet, leaving a space between the biscuits as they will spread a little, and flatten each biscuit slightly with the ball of your thumb, then using the tines of a fork, press on to the top of the biscuit to create lines. Bake for 10 minutes until pale and golden then leave the biscuits to cool on a wire rack while you make the ganache.

Smash the chocolate into gravel-sized pieces with a rolling pin (either leave the chocolate in its wrapper to do this or put it in a plastic bag). Heat the cream to just below boiling point, then place the chocolate into a heatproof bowl and pour over the hot cream. Gently stir until all the chocolate has melted. As the ganache cools it will thicken. When it is a spreadable consistency, sandwich 2 biscuits together keeping the lined edges on the outside.

Finally dust the biscuits with icing sugar.

Chocolate and ginger lovelies

Not to be confused with the Ginger Shortbread with Darkest Chocolate on page 253, these biscuits aren't particularly sophisticated, but chocolate and ginger go together like the old yin and yang, so we must obey the rules and have plenty of delicious biscuits.

✳ Makes 1 batch

125 g/4½ oz/9 tbsp butter, softened
85 g/3½ oz/scant ½ cup soft light brown sugar
1 tbsp golden (corn) syrup
1 large free-range egg yolk
200 g/7 oz/scant 1½ cups plain (all-purpose) flour, plus extra for dusting
25 g/1 oz/¼ cup cocoa powder
2 tsp ground ginger
1 tsp bicarbonate of soda (baking soda)
100 g/4 oz milk or dark chocolate (optional)

Preheat the oven to 190°C/375°F/Gas Mark 5 and line 2 baking sheets with silicone liners.

Beat the butter and sugar together in a large bowl until pale and fluffy. Add the golden syrup and egg yolk and beat away. Sift the flour, cocoa, ginger and bicarbonate of soda over the butter mixture and mix it in until a dough forms. Knead the dough on a floured surface until smooth, then wrap in cling film and leave to chill in the refrigerator for at least 30 minutes – an hour would be better.

Pull little chunks of dough off and roll into little balls. Flatten them slightly and place on your lined baking sheets. Bake for about 10 minutes then transfer to a wire rack to cool.

When cold they are delicious as they are, but if you like, you can break the chocolate up into little pieces and melt in a heatproof bowl set over a pan of simmering water. Do not let the base of the bowl touch the water. When the chocolate has melted, drizzle it over the biscuits and leave to set.

Chocolate chip shortbread

This is a really easy peasy way of jazzing up shortbread.

✳ Makes 1 batch

1 batch Basic Shortbread
 dough (see p.191)
50 g/2 oz/¼ cup chunky
 chocolate chips

Make the dough according to the instructions on page 191.
Sprinkle the chocolate chips over the dough and knead
in with your lovely clean hands until the chocolate is
evenly distributed.

Roll out a sheet of cling film, tip the dough on to it, then form
the dough into a fat sausage and wrap up tightly. Leave to
chill in the refrigerator for at least an hour.

Preheat the oven to 170°C/325°F/Gas Mark 3 and line
2 baking sheets with silicone liners.

Remove the roll of dough from its cling film and slice into
rounds. Place the rounds on your lined baking sheets and
bake for about 30 minutes until they are pale golden. Leave
the shortbread to cool on wire racks.

What-a-lotta-chocca

You have to have one recipe for biscuits containing all three sorts of chocolate, surely? Some may see it as chocolate overload. I see it as entirely acceptable and not needing any form of admission of greed. It does, however, require a gargantuan amount of chocolate and this alone may make these biscuits the stuff of 'treats' rather than everyday indulgences.

✳ Makes 1 batch

125 g/4½ oz/scant 1 cup plain (all-purpose) flour
½ tsp bicarbonate of soda (baking soda)
25 g/1 oz/generous ¼ cup cocoa powder
125 g/4½ oz good-quality dark chocolate
85 g/3½ oz/7 tbsp butter, softened
175 g/6 oz/scant 1 cup soft light brown sugar
2 large free-range eggs
1 tsp vanilla extract
350 g/12 oz/2 cups milk chocolate chips
55 g/2 oz white chocolate chunks

Preheat the oven to 180°C/350°F/Gas Mark 4 and line 2 baking sheets with silicone liners.

Sift the flour, bicarbonate of soda and cocoa into a large bowl and set aside. Break the dark chocolate up into little pieces and melt in a heatproof bowl set over a pan of simmering water. Do not let the base of the bowl touch the water. Let it cool slightly.

Cream the butter and sugar together in another large bowl until light and fluffy, then beat in the eggs and the vanilla extract. Stir the melted chocolate into the mixture, then the milk and white chocolate chunks. Fold all of this gooey mess into the flour mix and drop small spoonfuls of the mixture on to your lined baking sheets, leaving good gaps between them. Bake for 10 minutes then leave them on their sheets to harden slightly before transferring them to wire racks to cool. You may wish to stand over the biscuits and inhale deeply at this stage. Up to you.

Chocolate nutters

Do you like peanut butter sandwiches? You do? Oh good. May I suggest these as the next move towards peanut indulgence? Really yummy and very little effort is required.

✳ **Makes 1 batch**

110 g/4 oz/8 tbsp butter, softened
110 g/4 oz/½ cup soft light
   brown sugar
50 g/2 oz crunchy peanut butter
1 large free-range egg
275 g/10 oz/2 cups plain
   (all-purpose) flour
200 g/7 oz dark or milk chocolate

Preheat the oven to 190°C/375°F/Gas Mark 5 and line 2 baking sheets with silicone liners.

Cream the butter and sugar together in a large bowl until light and fluffy. Beat in the peanut butter and the egg, then fold in the flour.

Take 50 g/2 oz of the chocolate and bash it into gravel-sized chunks (or whatever size you like your chocolate pieces to be) and knead them into the dough. Take little blobs of the dough and form into a ball and then flatten them into biscuit shapes. Place them on your lined baking sheets and bake for about 10–12 minutes until golden. Transfer the biscuits to a wire rack to cool.

Break the remaining chocolate up into little pieces and melt in a heatproof bowl set over a pan of simmering water. Do not let the base of the bowl touch the water. Then using a spoon drizzle the melted chocolate over the cold biscuits. Leave the chocolate to set and harden before launching in.

Chocolate orange biscuits
à la Thierry

Those of you familiar with British confectionery shelves will recognize a product called the Terry's Chocolate Orange™. You will need one of these beauties here. If you live in more exotic climes, then get your hands on some chocolate flavoured with orange oil.

✳ Makes 1 batch

125 g/4½ oz/9 tbsp butter, softened
200 g/7 oz/1 cup caster sugar
1 large free-range egg
Finely grated zest of 1 large orange
225 g/8 oz/1⅔ cups plain (all-purpose) flour
1 tsp baking powder
3 tbsp cocoa powder
175 g/6 oz Terry's Chocolate Orange™ or 175 g/6 oz of orange chocolate

Preheat the oven to 190°C/375°F/Gas Mark 5 and line 2 baking sheets with silicone liners.

Cream the butter and sugar in a large bowl until pale and fluffy. Add the egg and orange zest and beat well. Sift over the flour, baking powder and cocoa and give it a good mix.

Now for the interesting bit. For those with the actual Chocolate Orange (hoorah!) tap it, unwrap it ... no, no, really, be serious now, and smash it to bits with a rolling pin. Gravel-sized chunks are required here. For those with a bar of chocolate, just smash it up, will you? Mix the chocolate into the biscuit mixture, then take spoonfuls of the mixture, form them into balls and plop them on your lined baking trays, leaving a little space between them as they spread. Bake for about 15 minutes, then transfer them to a wire rack to cool. Terry would be so proud.

Coleman cookies

These gorgeous chocolate chip cookies are called Coleman Cookies after my friend Claire who gave me the recipe. It is the sort of foolproof, wonderful stand-by recipe to have at your fingertips when you want one of those big, spreading, softish cookies, full of hunks of yummy chocolate. And you want it fast. Marvellous.

✳ Makes 1 batch

125 g/4½ oz/9 tbsp butter
175 g/6 oz/scant 1 cup soft light brown sugar
1 large free-range egg
1 tsp vanilla extract
150 g/5 oz/generous 1 cup plain (all-purpose) flour
½ tsp baking powder
Pinch of salt (omit if using salted butter)
100 g/4 oz white, milk or dark chocolate, chopped into largish chunks

Preheat the oven to 180°C/350°F/Gas Mark 5 and line 2 baking sheets with silicone liners.

Melt the butter in a large saucepan, then add the sugar and take the pan off the heat. Beat in the egg, add the vanilla extract, then sift in the dry ingredients, giving it a good old stir so that you don't start cooking that egg. Stir in the chocolate chunks.

These babies spread, so leave a good gap when you spoon little piles on to your lined baking sheets. Bake for about 10 minutes. Leave for a few minutes to settle before sliding them on to a wire rack to cool. Do the decent thing and at least pretend that you are going to leave them to get cold...

Choccy melts

Now these are genius biscuits. They don't look hugely exciting, but take a bite and wow, they really do melt in the mouth and are utterly, utterly delicious. I love them because if you make them at the same time as something very flashy, everyone ignores these. I get quite jittery when people's hands hover over these brown nuggets of joy. Oh the relief when they decide on a Rocky Road (see page 246) instead. And they are easy peasy to make. Genius, I tell you, genius.

✳ Makes 1 batch

125 g/4½ oz/9 tbsp butter, softened
50 g/2 oz/½ cup icing (confectioners') sugar, sifted
50 g/2 oz/2 cups cornflour (cornstarch)
25 g/1 oz/¼ cup cocoa powder
100 g/4 oz/¾ cup plain (all-purpose) flour
100 g/4 oz dark or milk chocolate

Preheat the oven to 190°C/375°F/Gas Mark 5 and line 2 baking sheets with silicone liners.

Beat the butter in a large bowl until very soft, then simply add all the other ingredients except for the 100 g/4 oz of chocolate. Mix together (easier to get your hands in, I think) until it forms a dough. Take small balls of the dough and flatten them slightly until you are happy with the size and shape. Place them on your lined baking sheets and bake for about 10–12 minutes. Leave the biscuits to cool on the baking sheets as the silicone liners are very handy for the next bit.

Break the chocolate up into little pieces and melt in a heat-proof bowl set over a pan of simmering water. Do not let the base of the bowl touch the water. When the chocolate has melted, use a spoon to drizzle it all over the biscuits then leave to set on the lined sheets.

When the chocolate has set, the finished biscuits are really easy to pick off the liners. No mess. Sorted. Hands off. They're mine.

No mucking around chocolate macaroons

I am not known for my willingness to hold back on culinary extras. Plain and simple is anathema to me. When I started experimenting with a recipe for chocolate macaroons, I anticipated that I would sandwich them together with a rich ganache for a gloriously over-the-top treat. Well, I made the macaroons (about 20 times before I was happy, but you needn't lose any sleep over that ...) and then the strangest thing happened. They were just so lovely as they were that, for once, I decided to leave well alone. Feel free, though, to sandwich the little lovelies together with something glorious. I will understand.

✳ Makes 24

2 large egg whites
1 tbsp caster (superfine) sugar
75 g/2¾ oz/generous ⅔ cup
   ground almonds
2 tbsp cocoa powder
   (unsweetened cocoa)
125 g/4½ oz/1¼ cups icing
   (confectioners') sugar, sifted
½ tsp almond extract
24 almonds

Line two baking sheets with silicone liners; the macaroons will stick to anything else. The only other alternative is edible rice paper. Preheat the oven to 180°C/350°F/Gas Mark 4.

In a large, clean bowl, whisk the egg whites until they form soft peaks. Then add the caster (superfine) sugar and whisk again until the mixture is really stiff and shiny. Fold in the ground almonds, cocoa, icing (confectioners') sugar and the almond extract. Put the mixture into a piping (pastry) bag fitted with a plain nozzle (tip). Pipe small circles onto the baking sheets with lots of space between each blob, and pop an almond on top of each one. Bake for about 10 minutes, or until set and golden.

Transfer to a wire rack to cool. Crispy the first day and then deliciously chewy after that.

Biscotti with the choccolotti

These are delicious served with a creamy dessert – or even just a dollop of mascarpone, some raspberries and a glass of dessert wine. By the way, they keep for ages in an airtight tin.

✳ Makes one batch

125 g/4½ oz/generous ¾ cup whole almonds
100 g/3½ oz/3½ squares plain (bittersweet) chocolate, chopped into gravel-sized chunks
250 g/9 oz/1⅔ cups plain (all-purpose) flour
2 tbsp cocoa powder (unsweetened cocoa)
150 g/5½ oz/¾ cup caster (superfine) sugar
1 tsp baking powder
3 large eggs

Preheat the oven to 180°C/350°F/Gas Mark 4 and line two baking sheets with silicone liners. Chop the almonds very roughly – don't chop them too small.

In a large bowl, mix all the ingredients, apart from the eggs. Lightly beat the eggs, then stir them in until you form a cohesive ball of dough. I use my hands, which is much easier. If the dough is a bit too sticky, just add more flour until you are happy.

Halve the ball of dough and form it into two flat loaf shapes about 3 cm/1 in high and 20 cm/8 in long. Place the loaves onto the baking sheets and bake for about 20 minutes, or until cooked through. Remove the loaves and leave to cool. Do not turn off the oven.

When the loaves are cool, cut each into slices 5 mm/¼ in thick and place the slices back onto the baking sheets. Return to the oven for 10 minutes. Then take them out, flip them over and return to the oven for another 5 minutes. Transfer the biscotti to a wire rack to cool before putting them in an airtight tin.

Biscotti

I think these are really versatile little biscuits. They are very easy to make, you can play around with the flavourings by leaving ingredients out, putting little extras in ... change the nuts, dried fruit, add chocolate – they are a truly forgiving biscuit! The other wonderful thing they have going for them is that they are equally happy being served with morning coffee, as a dunking device with a pudding or even as a *petit four* with dark, strong coffee and a small glass of something after dinner.

✳ Makes 1 batch

125 g/4½ oz/generous ¾ cup
   whole almonds
100 g/4 oz/generous ½ cup
   dried ready-to-eat apricots
250 g/9 oz/1¾ cups plain
   (all-purpose) flour
150 g/5 oz/¾ cup caster
   (superfine) sugar
1 tsp baking powder
3 large free-range eggs

Preheat the oven to 180°C/350°F/Gas Mark 4 and line 2 baking sheets with silicone liners.

Chop the almonds and apricots into manageable-sized chunks, then mix them in well with all the ingredients except for the eggs in a large bowl. Add the eggs and stir to combine (get your hands in there) until you have a dough that comes together into a ball. If the mixture is a bit sticky, add a smidgen more flour until you are happy with the consistency.

Halve the ball of dough and shape each half into long, flat loaf shapes about 3 cm/1¼ inches high and 20 cm/8 inches long. Place the loaves on your lined baking sheets and bake for about 20 minutes until very pale gold and cooked through. Don't turn the oven off!

Leave to cool for a moment or two and when you can handle them, cut each loaf into 5 mm/¼ inch thick slices (don't get a ruler out, please) and place these slices back on to the baking sheets. Return to the oven for 10 more minutes, then turn them over and cook for another 5 minutes. Transfer the slices to a wire rack to cool. These keep really well in an airtight tin.

Safe as houses chocolate digestives

The digestive is a homely, comforting, reassuring sort of biscuit. A chocolate digestive is all of the above but with the extra bonus that takes it from "everyday" to "wey-hey". Use milk or plain (bittersweet) chocolate – it doesn't matter. I would add, though, that there is a very good reason you don't get white chocolate digestives in the shops. Nasty.

✳ Makes one batch

100 g/3½ oz/scant ⅔ cup wholemeal (whole-wheat) flour
40 g/1½ oz/scant ⅓ cup plain (all-purpose) flour, plus extra for dusting
½ tsp baking powder
1 tbsp oats
120 g/4¼ oz/generous 1 stick butter, softened
100 g/3½ oz/½ cup (solidly packed) soft light brown sugar
4 tbsp milk
200 g/7 oz/7 squares milk or plain (bittersweet) chocolate

Preheat the oven to 190°C/375°F/Gas Mark 5 and line two baking sheets with silicone liners.

Mix the flours, baking powder and oats together in a large bowl. In another bowl, cream the butter and sugar together until pale and fluffy, then add the flour mixture to this. Add the milk a little at a time, until you have a thick dough.

Turn the dough out on to a lightly floured surface and give it a quick knead, until it's lovely and smooth, then roll it out to about 3 mm/⅛ in thick and cut into discs. Place the discs onto the baking sheets and prick them all over with a fork. Bake for 15 minutes, or until golden.

Transfer the biscuits to a wire rack to cool. When they are cold, melt the chocolate according to your preferred method, then spread the chocolate onto one side of the biscuit. Leave chocolate side up to set.

Butterscotch chocolate chip cookies

This recipe came about after having a fiddle around with one of my all-time favourite cookie recipes. It's quick, it's easy and uses stuff that you generally have knocking around in the kitchen cupboard. A plan with no drawbacks.

✳ Makes one batch – you might make them huge, you might make them tiny...

125 g/4½ oz/generous 1 stick butter
175 g/6 oz/scant 1 cup (solidly packed) soft light brown sugar
1 large egg
1 tsp vanilla extract
150 g/5½ oz/1 cup plain (all-purpose) flour
½ tsp baking powder
200 g/7 oz milk chocolate chunks

Preheat the oven to 180°C/350°F/Gas Mark 4 and line two baking sheets with silicone liners.

Melt the butter in a large saucepan. Add the sugar and stir it around until the sugar has dissolved and the mixture starts bubbling, then take it off the heat immediately. Beat the mixture to cool it down a little, then add the egg, beating it in quickly. Add first the vanilla, then the flour and baking powder. Once everything is well combined, add the chocolate and give it another quick stir.

Take small spoonfuls of the mixture and plop them onto the baking sheet, leaving masses of room between each blob to allow for spreading. Bake for about 10 minutes. Leave the cookies on the baking sheet to firm up for a few minutes, then transfer to a wire rack to cool completely.

Rocky road cookies

I love Rocky Road – you know the stuff: melted chocolate, crushed biscuits, marshmallows and all sorts of other goodies. While researching this book, I found a recipe for 'Rocky Road Cookies'. The excitement was almost unbearable and I whizzed off to the kitchen to make them. Inedible and really, really disgusting. The disappointment was crushing. But the seed had been sown, so may I present my version of the Rocky Road Cookie? All the requirements are here – chocolate, biscuit, marshmallow and my own addition of hazelnuts, which I think is particularly gorgeous.

✳ Makes 1 batch

1 batch Rich Tea biscuits
  (see p.192)
300 g/10 oz milk chocolate
200 g/7 oz mini marshmallows
100 g/4 oz/⅔ cup hazelnuts

Make the Rich Tea biscuits according to the instructions on page 192 (don't forget to use unsalted butter) and let them cool.

Break the chocolate up into little pieces and melt in a heat-proof bowl set over a pan of simmering water. Do not let the base of the bowl touch the water. When the chocolate has melted, stir in the marshmallows and hazelnuts.

Lay the biscuits on a wire rack and carefully spoon a mound of the chocolate mixture on top. You can create quite a mound, depending on your greed. Try and leave a little edge of naked biscuit all the way round. You *have* to leave them to set and harden. Sorry. But you do. Go and clear out the cutlery drawer or sort out the airing cupboard. Go on. Go.

Fig rolls

I love them, but admit they are a bit fiddly to make. That is why this recipe makes a rather massive amount of filling and dough, but I have purposefully done this – make them and freeze them uncooked. It takes no longer to make double the amount and you can pluck a couple out of the freezer any time you want – quick blast in the oven and *voilà*! Just to let you know, my love of fig rolls is shared by my family. When my mother and sister were here, they were on their second one before they stopped, almost in unison, looked more carefully at the biscuit, then looked at me and said, 'Did you make these?' Result (as my son would say).

✳ Makes 2 batches

200 g/7 oz/scant 1 cup white vegetable fat
300 g/10 oz/1½ cups caster (superfine) sugar
3 large free-range eggs
1 tsp vanilla extract
500 g/1 lb 2 oz/3½ cups plain (all-purpose) flour, plus extra for dusting
1 tsp baking powder
A little milk (optional)

Filling:
250 g/9 oz dried figs
100 g/4 oz pitted dates
100 g/4 oz dried pears
1 small apple, cored and quartered
2 tbsp water (optional)

Make the dough first. Cream the vegetable fat and sugar together in a large bowl. This is a bit of a palaver and you'll need to keep scraping down the bowl, but stick with it. Add the eggs and vanilla and beat them in. You'll end up with a mess looking like scrambled eggs. Don't panic. Sift in the flour and baking powder and mix it in. At this stage I like to empty it out of the bowl on to a floured surface and give it a good knead. If the dough is too sticky, keep adding sprinklings of flour and kneading until you get a consistency you are happy with. If the dough is too dry, add a spot of milk.

Wrap the dough in cling film and leave to chill in the refrigerator.

To make the filling, you really need a food processor (or a sharp knife and lots of patience). Blitz the figs, dates, pears and apple until you have a chunky-ish paste. If it's all too stiff, add the water to loosen it up a bit. Keep blitzing until it is as smooth as possible (it will never be as smooth as the shop-bought version).

Preheat the oven to 190°C/375°F/Gas Mark 5 and line 2 baking sheets with silicone liners.

Roll out the dough on a well-floured surface until it is about 3 mm/⅛ inch thick – you may choose to do this in 2 stages. Cut the dough into 8 cm/3 inch strips, then create a chipolata-sized long sausage of filling all the way down the strip of dough, about 1.5 cm/⅝ inch from one edge. I use my hands for this, but it is up to you. Wipe a little water down the long edge of the dough next to the filling, take the non-wet edge and fold it over the filling and then take the wet edge and seal that sausage. Cut the roll into manageable-sized pieces and place, sealed edged downwards, on to your lined baking sheets.

Bake the rolls for about 15 minutes until pale golden, then leave to cool on a wire rack. Stop baking when you've got enough for the biscuit tin and freeze the rest of the uncooked fig rolls in their cut state.

Tiramisu bars

I have to admit to feeling a bit sheepish about this recipe. Is it really a biscuit? The other heinous crime is that it includes bought biscuits – a double whammy of naughtiness. Please don't write letters, I am fully aware. On the plus side, they are extraordinarily good. Very, very rich and very, very adult.

✳ Makes 1 batch

200 g/7 oz amaretti biscuits, crushed
2 tsp instant espresso coffee granules
80 g/3½ oz/7 tbsp butter, melted
250 g/9 oz/generous 1 cup cream cheese
50 g/2 oz/¼ cup caster (superfine) sugar
2 large free-range eggs
60 ml/2½ fl oz/generous ¼ cup double (heavy) cream
55 ml/2 fl oz/¼ cup rum
1 tsp vanilla extract
100 g/4 oz dark chocolate (at least 70% cocoa solids)
100 ml/3½ fl oz/generous ⅓ cup double (heavy) cream
50g/2 oz/¼ cup chocolate coffee beans (optional)

Preheat the oven to 180°C/350°F/Gas Mark 4 and line a 23 cm/9 inch square tin with greaseproof paper or a silicone liner.

Mix the amaretti biscuit crumbs with the dry coffee granules and the melted butter until well incorporated and then press the mixture into the bottom of the tin. Give it a really good firm pressing. Leave to set and harden in the refrigerator while you make the rest of the biscuit.

In a large bowl, beat the cream cheese with the sugar, eggs, cream, rum and vanilla. Pour the mixture over the biscuit base and bake for 20–25 minutes or until the centre is set. Leave to cool in the tin.

Make the topping by smashing the chocolate into gravel-sized chunks and placing in a heatproof bowl. Heat the cream in a pan until it is just about to come to the boil, then take it off the heat and pour it over the chocolate. Leave for a minute or so, then gently stir to melt the chocolate and amalgamate everything. Pour the ganache over the top of the cheesecake, scatter the chocolate coffee beans over the top (if using) and leave to set for 30 minutes. Cover with cling film and chill in the refrigerator for at least an hour until firm. Cut into squares and serve.

Ginger shortbread
with darkest chocolate

Unlike the chocolate ginger biscuits in the chocolate chapter, these are definitely for grown-ups. They are a sophisticated little number with chunks of crystallized ginger 'embedded' in 'luxurious' all-butter shortbread, 'enrobed' or should I say 'draped' in the darkest chocolate. Ooooh. I've come over all 'menu-speak'. Down the hatch...

✴ Makes 1 batch

1 batch Basic Shortbread dough
   (see p.191)
100 g/4 oz crystallized
   (preserved) ginger, chopped
   into small pieces
100 g/4 oz dark chocolate
   (at least 70% cocoa solids)

Make the shortbread according to the instructions on page 191 and when you reach the dough stage, add the ginger and knead it in until it is evenly distributed. Roll the dough into a large sausage and wrap it in cling film. Leave to chill in the refrigerator for at least 30 minutes, longer if possible. If you are short of time, bung it in the freezer for 15 minutes.

Preheat the oven to 190°C/375°F/Gas Mark 5 and line 2 baking sheets with silicone liners.

Unwrap the ginger log, slice off 5 mm/¼ inch pieces and place on your lined baking sheets. Bake for 12–15 minutes until golden round the edges. Transfer the slices to a wire rack to cool.

When they are cold, melt the chocolate in a heatproof bowl set over a pan of simmering water. Do not let the base of the bowl touch the water. I place the biscuits back onto the silicone liners at this stage. Pick up a biscuit and holding it over the bowl of melted chocolate, spoon the chocolate over half the biscuit so that the drips fall back into the bowl. Place the biscuit on the silicone liner and leave to set. It's much easier to peel them off this stuff than wrestle with the rack.

Grown up, proper, special occasion macaroons

These are truly a world away from the lurid humdingers that are coconut macaroons. No coconut in sight, and not even any colouring, just lovely delicate morsels, slightly crispy on the outside, chewy and moist on the inside, and a wonderful excuse to eat chocolate ganache. Heaven.

✳ Makes 1 batch (not a
   huge batch...)

2 large free-range egg whites
140 g/5 oz/¾ cup caster
   (superfine) sugar
80 g/3½ oz/scant 1 cup
   ground almonds
100 ml/3½ fl oz/generous
   ⅓ cup double (heavy) cream
100 g/4 oz dark chocolate
   (at least 70% cocoa solids)

Preheat the oven to 180°C/350°F/Gas Mark 4 and line 2 baking sheets with silicone liners (crucial).

Whisk the egg whites until very stiff then gradually sprinkle the sugar over the egg whites and whisk away before adding the next sprinkling. I usually aim to use up the sugar in 4 or 5 batches. Sprinkle the almonds over the meringue mix (all at once is fine) and gently fold them in. Plonk the mixture into a large piping bag fitted with a plain wide nozzle (about 1 cm/½ inch) and pipe small rounds on to your lined baking trays. You don't really want any swirly flourishes here. Keep them sensible. Bake for about 12 minutes, but don't let them burn. They should be just about set and have turned a little more golden. Burnt almond doesn't taste good at all. I leave them to cool on their trays.

To make the ganache, heat the cream in a pan until it is just about to come to the boi,l then take it off the heat immediately. Smash the chocolate to gravel-sized chunks and place in a heatproof bowl. Pour the hot cream over the chocolate and leave alone for a minute, then stir gently to melt the chocolate and amalgamate everything. As the ganache cools it thickens. When it is a spreadable consistency, carefully take a macaroon, spread a blob of ganache on to it, and sandwich another macaroon on top. Leave to set – if you can.

Lemon snaps

I love these delicate little lemony biscuits. They seem rather genteel and should be nibbled at, rather than scoffed. Lovely with a cup of tea and also really good with puddings of the syllabub variety.

✳ Makes 1 batch

125 g/4½ oz/9 tbsp butter, softened
125 g/4½ oz/scant ⅔ cup caster (superfine) sugar
3 large free-range egg whites
Finely grated zest of 2 large lemons
125 g/4½ oz/scant 1 cup plain (all-purpose) flour

Preheat the oven to 200°C/400°F/Gas Mark 6 and line 2 baking sheets with silicone liners.

Beat the butter and sugar together in a large bowl until pale and fluffy. In a separate bowl, whisk the egg whites until very stiff then fold them into the butter and sugar mixture. This is actually quite tricky, but keep going, it's possible! Add the lemon zest and mix until combined. Sift the flour over the bowl and fold into the mixture.

Take small teaspoons of the mixture and blob them on to your lined baking trays, leaving plenty of space between them, then with the back of the spoon, flatten the blobs and spread them around in a circular-type manner. Bake for 5–6 minutes until the biscuits are golden around the edges. Leave them on the trays for a few moments to set a little before transferring them to a wire rack to cool.

You may well find that you have to cook these biscuits in several batches, as you can't fit many on a tray due to them spreading. It's not too arduous – they are very quick to cook.

Cardamom and white chocolate shortbread

Sounds weird, but tastes good! These biscuits are gently fragranced and go very well with puddings or just a cup of tea (Earl Grey of course).

✴ Makes 1 batch

1 batch Basic Shortbread dough
  (see p.191)
6 cardamom pods
50 g/2 oz white chocolate chunks
2 tsp orange flower water
  (optional)
100 g/4 oz white chocolate

Start by making up the dough according to the instructions on page 191, but leave it in the mixing bowl.

Gently split the cardamom pods, remove the tiny seeds and discard the outer husks. Use a pestle and mortar or the back of a teaspoon on a saucer to crush the seeds to a fine powder.

Add the ground cardamom, the chocolate chunks and the orange flower water (if using) to the dough and knead well to make sure everything is evenly distributed. Lay out a sheet of cling film, tip the dough on to it and form the dough into a fat sausage and wrap tightly. Leave to chill in the refrigerator for at least an hour.

Preheat the oven to 170°C/375°F/Gas Mark 5 and line 2 baking sheets with silicone liners.

Remove the dough from the cling film and slice into rounds about 1 cm/½ inch thick. Place the rounds on your lined baking sheets and bake for 25–30 minutes until pale golden. Transfer to a wire rack to cool.

When the biscuits are cold, melt the remaining white chocolate in a heatproof bowl set over a pan of simmering water. Do not let the base of the bowl touch the water. Take a teaspoon of chocolate and drizzle over the top of the biscuits. This sets really quickly so you can start scoffing before too long!

Millionaire's shortbread

I love the idea of a bunch of millionaires sitting round, taking tea, discussing their pots of money, a cigar in one hand and reaching for their shortbread with another. They would certainly be discussing the legal position of prohibiting those with limited funds from eating such a delicacy. This shortbread *must* be consumed by millionaires only. What I want to know is, what do *billionaires* eat?

※ Makes 12–24 depending on how you cut it

For the shortbread
250 g/9 oz/2¼ sticks butter, softened, plus extra for greasing
50 g/1¾ oz/¼ cup caster (superfine) sugar
250 g/9 oz/1⅔ cups plain (all-purpose) flour
125 g/4½ oz/scant 1 cup cornflour (cornstarch)

For the caramel
175 g/6 oz/1½ sticks butter
175 g/6 oz/scant 1 cup caster (superfine) sugar
4 tbsp golden (corn) syrup
1 x 400 g/14 oz tin (can) condensed milk

For the topping
350 g/12 oz/12 squares chocolate (milk or plain/bittersweet)

Preheat the oven to 170°C/325°F/Gas Mark 3. Line a 28 x 20 cm/11 x 8 in tin (pan) with silicone liner.

First make the shortbread. Cream the butter and sugar together until pale and fluffy. Stir in the flour and cornflour (cornstarch) and combine till you have a smooth, pasty dough. Press the mixture into the tin, squishing it right to the edges and getting a smooth surface. Prick with a fork and then bake for 20 minutes, or until pale golden brown. Leave in the tin to cool.

For the caramel, put the butter, sugar, syrup and condensed milk into a heavy pan and slowly, over a gentle heat, melt the mixture, stirring frequently. Once it has melted, bring it up to a gentle bubble and keep stirring. Do not stop stirring and be aware that the molten bubbling mass will spit at you when you are least expecting it. After about 5 minutes, it will be thicker and golden. Carefully tip the caramel over the shortbread. Leave for about 30 minutes to set a bit.

Melt the chocolate, then pour it over the caramel and place the shortbread in the refrigerator for 1–2 hours. When the chocolate has set, carefully cut it into squares as big or small as you want – don't forget, it's for millionaires, so it's rich. Try not to cut your beloved silicone liner.

Liberty Florentines

I've taken liberties with this recipe! Traditionally, Florentines contain almonds (yum), raisins (yum), cherries (yum) and mixed peel (yuck). I can't make something with an ingredient that makes me want to wipe my tongue, so changes had to be made. And then I got all carried away and tropical...

✳ Makes 18–20

100 g/3½ oz/⅔ cup flaked (slivered) almonds
25 g/1 oz/¼ cup crystallized (candied) papaya
25 g/1 oz/¼ cup crystallized (candied) pineapple
25 g/1 oz/¼ cup crystallized (candied) ginger
25 g/1 oz/¼ cup glacé (candied) cherries
90 g/3¼ oz/generous ¾ stick butter
100 g/3½ oz/½ cup caster (superfine) sugar
50 g/2 oz/¼ cup plain (all-purpose) flour
1 tbsp double (heavy) cream
200 g/7 oz/7 squares chocolate, according to preference

Line three baking sheets with washable silicone liners or good-quality greaseproof (waxed) paper. Preheat the oven to 180°C/350°F/Gas Mark 4.

Roughly chop the almonds and the fruit. Melt the butter and the sugar over a low heat in a heavy-based pan. Turn up the heat and boil vigorously for 1 minute, stirring now and then. Remove from the heat and cool. Stir in the flour, then the cream, followed by the chopped fruit and nuts. Stir to combine.

Take small teaspoonfuls of the mixture and plop onto the baking sheets, leaving plenty of space between them. (I tell you, these babies spread.) Bake for 10 minutes, or until golden brown.

Remove from the oven. If you don't like the shape, take a spatula and push the sides around the Florentine to neaten. Leave alone on the tray for about 5 minutes to start firming up, then lift onto a wire rack to cool completely.

Melt your chocolate according to your preferred method, then leave to cool for about 10 minutes. Just as it is starting to thicken and is less runny, take a palette knife and spread the base of the Florentines with the chocolate, then place back onto the baking sheet to set, with the chocolate side up.

Apricot and almond rugelach

As I understand it, Rugelach are traditional Jewish holiday biscuits, but the addition of cream cheese in the dough is an American tradition. Rugelach can have any number of fillings – hazelnuts, poppy seeds, raisins – I've plumped for apricot and almond here. There's some minor fiddling to be done, but the pastry is really easy to make and freezes beautifully.

✳ Makes 1 batch

115 g/4 oz/8 tbsp butter, cubed
125 g/4½ oz/scant 1 cup plain (all-purpose) flour, plus extra for dusting
115 g/4 oz/½ cup cream cheese
50 g/2 oz/¼ cup caster (superfine) sugar
70 g/2¾ oz/½ cup toasted and chopped almonds
Finely grated zest of 1 large unwaxed lemon
240 g/9 oz apricot jam
1 large free-range egg, beaten
30 g/1 oz/scant ¼ cup chopped almonds
Icing (confectioners') sugar, for dusting

Make the pastry first. I find it easier to bung it in a food processor – blitz the butter and flour together and when you've got to the crumb stage, add the cream cheese, blitz again, and hey presto – dough. If you are doing it by hand, rub the butter into the flour until you get to breadcrumb stage then knead in the cream cheese until you form a ball of sticky dough. Split the dough in half, wrap both balls in cling film and pop them in the refrigerator for a couple of hours.

To make the fillings, simply combine the sugar, toasted almonds and lemon zest. To assemble the whole caboodle, place 1 ball of dough on a well-floured surface, it's much easier to do this one ball at a time, believe me, and roll out the dough into a round at least 25 cm/10 inches in diameter. Spread apricot jam all over the round of dough then sprinkle half the sugar, lemon and nut mixture over the round. Cut the round into 12 wedges then roll up each wedge from the wider outside edge, rolling up towards the middle. Bend each little wedge to make a crescent and place on your lined baking sheet. When you have your 12 rolled up, brush them with a little beaten egg and sprinkle with half the chopped almonds. Bake for about 20–25 minutes at 180°C/350°F/Gas Mark 4, until they are golden brown. While they are in the oven, you can repeat with the second ball of dough. Once all the rugelach are cooked and cooled, dust with a little icing sugar.

Spekulatius

When I was chatting to some friends about this book, I muttered about needing some really Christmassy biscuits. Dominic's ears pricked up, what with him having a German mother and all that. So thank you Dominic and Mama Naegele for all your recipes and I'm only sorry there's just room for one here. The name of this particular recipe, I am reliably informed by the *hausfrau* herself, comes from the word 'speculum' (mirror) because they used to be made in shallow, carved wooden forms of which, after taking them out, they show the mirror image. So there you have it.

✳ Makes 1 batch

150 g/5 oz/10 tbsp butter
125 g/4½ oz/scant ⅔ cup soft
    light brown sugar
1 large free-range egg
1 tsp ground cinnamon
Largish pinch of ground cloves
Largish pinch of ground
    cardamom
Finely grated zest of ½ lemon
50 g/2 oz/½ cup ground almonds
300 g/10 oz/scant 2¼ cups
    self-raising (self-rising) flour,
    plus extra for dusting
50 g/2 oz/½ cup flaked
    (slivered) almonds
1 batch lemon glacé icing
    (see p.17) and gold dragées (op-
    tional), to decorate

Beat the butter and sugar together in a large bowl until pale and fluffy. Add the egg and thrash away. Add the spices, lemon zest and ground almonds and blend well. Add the flour and mix to form a dough. Roll the dough into a ball and wrap in cling film before chilling in the refrigerator for about an hour.

Preheat the oven to 200°C/400°F/Gas Mark 6 and line 2 baking sheets with silicone liners.

Roll the dough out on a floured surface to about 3 mm/ ⅛ inch thick and cut out shapes with whatever cutters you like. Sprinkle the flaked almonds on top of the biscuits and give them a gentle press to help them stick. Bake for 20 minutes until they are golden and gorgeous, then transfer to a wire rack to cool.

If you require adornment (though this is not in Mama Naegele's instructions, so we're going off-piste here), when the biscuits are cold, drizzle some lemon icing over them from a teaspoon and then strew a few gold or silver dragées onto the wet icing. Leave the biscuits on the wire tray while the icing dries and get that *glühwein* on...

Norwegian pepper cookies

I love the idea of slipping unexpected ingredients into everyday items, like biscuits. Black pepper is just the job! The pepper doesn't make the biscuits savoury, but just adds that little frisson you get from experiencing something lovely, but just a little bit weird...

✳ Makes 1 batch

250 g/9 oz/generous 1 cup
 unsalted butter
225 g/8 oz/generous 1 cup
 caster (superfine) sugar
55 ml/2 fl oz/¼ cup double
 (heavy) cream
1 tbsp hot water
1 tsp bicarbonate of soda
 (baking soda)
6 cardamom pods
500 g/1 lb 2 oz/3½ cups plain
 (all-purpose) flour
1 tsp baking powder
1 tsp ground cinnamon
1 tsp ground black pepper

Cream the butter and sugar together in a large bowl until pale and fluffy, then beat in the cream.

In another bowl, mix the hot water and bicarbonate of soda together and add that to the mixture. Gently split open the cardamom pods, scrape out the little seeds and grind them finely in a pestle and mortar or with the back of a spoon on a firm surface.

Sift the flour, baking powder and the spices on to the mixture and knead to form a dough. Roll the dough into a large sausage and wrap in cling film. Leave to chill in the refrigerator for at least an hour to harden.

Preheat the oven to 190°C/375°F/Gas Mark 5 and line 2 baking sheets with silicone liners.

Unwrap the dough sausage then cut into thin slices and place them on the baking tray. Bake for 6–8 minutes until golden then transfer the biscuits to a wire rack to cool.

Superfood berry biscuits

These are just the most delicious, fruit-packed, oaty, soft cookies. They are easy to make and you can alter the fruit to whatever you can get your hands on. Health food stores and now most supermarkets sell a vast array of dried tropical fruit. I've made them with dried mangoes, raisins, figs, blueberries, pears – all work beautifully. If you want the 'super' in your berry biscuits though, you do need to add cranberries, blueberries or goji berries. This is based on what I have read in magazines and I have absolutely no scientific proof at all that these biscuits will make you live longer. Make them and eat them because you want to, not because you feel you ought to.

Makes 1 batch

60 ml/2½ fl oz/generous ¼ cup sunflower oil
75 g/3 oz/6 tbsp butter, softened
110 g/4 oz/½ cup soft light brown sugar
1 large free-range egg
½ tsp vanilla extract
100 g/4 oz/¾ cup jumbo oats
150 g/5 oz/scant 1 cup plain wholemeal (whole-wheat) flour
½ tsp bicarbonate of soda (baking soda)
½ tsp baking powder
½ tsp ground cinnamon
110 g/4 oz dried apple
25 g/1 oz cranberries
25 g/1 oz blueberries

Preheat the oven to 180°C/350°F/Gas Mark 4 and line 2 baking sheets with silicone liners.

Mix the sunflower oil, butter and sugar together in a large bowl. Beat in the egg and vanilla, then stir in the oats. Sift the flour, bicarbonate of soda, baking powder and cinnamon over the sugar and oil mixture and mix in. Add the dried fruit and stir until they are just combined.

Drop dessertspoonfuls of the mixture on to your lined baking sheets, leaving lots of space between them as they spread and bake for about 10 minutes until pale golden. Leave on the baking sheets to harden and set a bit before cooling on wire racks.

Maple cloud cookies

These cookies have a light and fluffy texture – something between a soft cookie and a muffin. I have included them because they are sugar free, and are suitable for those who are sugar-intolerant and diabetics, who often get ignored in the home-made biscuit department. Sugar substitutes can be found in all supermarkets nowadays. It's usually in the sugar aisle.

✳ Makes 1 batch

110 g/4 oz/8 tbsp butter, softened (although if push comes to shove you could use something like a soy margarine)
115 g/4 oz/½ cup sour cream
125 g/4½ oz apple, peeled and grated
2 large free-range eggs
1 tsp maple syrup
½ tsp vanilla extract
250 g/9 oz/1¾ cups plain (all-purpose) flour
65 g/2½ oz/⅓ cup sugar substitute
1 tsp bicarbonate of soda (baking soda)
1 tsp baking powder

Preheat the oven to 190°C/375°F/Gas Mark 5 and line 2 baking sheets with silicone liners.

Mix the butter, sour cream, apple, eggs, maple syrup and vanilla together in a large bowl. In another bowl, sift in the flour, sugar substitute, bicarbonate of soda and baking powder, then add the dry ingredients to the wet ingredients and mix very well. Drop dessertspoons of the mixture on to your lined baking sheets and bake for about 10 minutes until pale golden. Transfer the biscuits to wire racks to cool.

Incredibly healthy humdingers

This has got to be the ultimate in virtuous biscuits. Yet again, I am pushing the boundaries about what actually constitutes a biscuit. These aren't even cooked, for goodness' sake. There is not one ingredient here that a full-on health food addict would have a problem with, and they are actually great as sports snacks too, as they fill a gap and have lots of lovely slow-release sugar properties. Perfect.

✳ Makes 1 batch

125 g/4½ oz/½ cup
　　sunflower seeds
1 tbsp tahini (sesame seed paste)
50 g/2 oz/⅓ cup desiccated
　　(dry unsweetened) or
　　shredded coconut
1 tbsp runny honey
40 g/1½ oz wheatgerm
50 g/2 oz dates, pitted
　　and chopped

Bash the sunflower seeds a little in a mortar with a pestle or in a food processor. You just want to break them up a bit. Tip them into a large bowl and add all the other ingredients. Form the mixture (easier to do this in 2 portions) into a roll, wrap tightly in cling film and leave to chill in the refrigerator for a couple of hours. When you are ready, just slice pieces off. I think this one keeps better in the refrigerator than a tin.

Bananas-a-go-go cookies

Right, these little chaps are pretty cool. Really easy to make, they are sugar and wheat free, the fat is 'healthy' fat, and they are really banana-ry! They are soft cookies, so if you are waiting for them to crisp up, you may be waiting a while, and they are also best eaten on the day you make them.

✳ Makes 1 batch

3 ripe bananas
180 g/6½ oz pitted dates, chopped
160 g/5½ oz/1 cup rolled jumbo oats
80 ml/3 fl oz/⅓ cup sunflower oil
1 tsp vanilla extract

Preheat the oven to 180°C/350°F/Gas Mark 4 and line 2 baking sheets with silicone liners.

Mash the bananas in a large bowl, then add the dates, oats, sunflower oil and vanilla, and give it a good mix. Leave the mixture to stand for 15–20 minutes to firm up a little and for the oats to absorb some of the liquid.

Drop teaspoons of the mixture on to your lined baking sheets and flatten with the back of a spoon – they don't spread much, so the shape you make on the sheet will be the shape of the finished biscuit. Bake for 15–20 minutes then transfer to a wire rack to cool.

Chewy date cookies

Dates are just fantastic in cooking, and their intense sweetness means that you can reduce the amount of sugar you add to the recipe. These date lovelies still contain sugar, as it's important for the chewy factor. You can reduce the amount of sugar you use, but it will change the overall consistency. You could also use entirely wholemeal flour instead of a mixture of white and brown. It is up to you.

✳ Makes 1 batch

75 g/3 oz/6 tbsp butter, softened
140 g/5 oz/¾ cup soft light
    brown sugar
Finely grated zest of 1 large
    unwaxed lemon
1 large free-range egg
100 g/4 oz/¾ cup plain
    (all-purpose) flour
80 g/3½ oz/½ cup wholemeal
    (whole-wheat) flour
1 tsp baking powder
½ tsp grated nutmeg
1 tsp ground cinnamon
Pinch of salt
60 ml/2½ fl oz/generous ¼ cup
    milk (skimmed, if going for the
    healthiest version possible)
180 g/6½ oz pitted dates,
    chopped

Preheat the oven to 170°C/325°F/Gas Mark 3 and line 2 baking sheets with silicone liners.

Cream the butter and sugar together in a large bowl until light and fluffy, then add the zest and egg and beat away. In another bowl, sift together the flours, baking powder, nutmeg, cinnamon and salt. Add to the creamed mixture in alternate dollops with a little bit of milk and beat well between each addition. Finally stir in the dates. Drop round dessertspoons of the mixture on to your lined baking sheets, leaving space between them as they spread, and bake for 12–15 minutes until golden. Transfer the biscuits to wire racks to cool.

Peter Rabbit biscuits

Well, carrot biscuits really. Fruit and vegetables in one biscuit?
Can this be true? Yes, I tell you, yes. Not at all 'worthy'-tasting: carrot
and ginger, crystallized papaya, cinnamon and a little hint of coconut,
all make these truly delicious little morsels. I'm just going to have
another one actually...

✻ Makes 1 batch

200 g/7 oz raw carrots, peeled
   and chopped
110 g/4 oz/8 tbsp hard white
   vegetable fat
110 g/4 oz/8 tbsp butter, softened
130 g/4¾ oz/¾ cup soft light
   brown sugar
1 large free-range egg
300 g/10 oz/scant 2¼ cups plain
   (all-purpose) flour
1 tsp baking powder
1 tsp ground cinnamon
1 tsp ground ginger
80 g/3½ oz/½ cup desiccated (dry
   unsweetened) or shredded coconut
50 g/2 oz crystallized (candied) papaya

Cook the carrots in a pan of unsalted boiling water until
tender and then purée in a blender. You need to avoid any
lumps at all, so push it through a sieve if you are unsure
whether your purée is smooth enough. Leave to cool
until cold.

Preheat the oven to 200°C/400°F/Gas Mark 6 and line
2 baking sheets with silicone liners.

Beat the white fat, butter and sugar together in a large
bowl. You may need to scrape the white fat off the bowl
every now and again, as it does like to stick to the sides.
When the mixture is looking pale and fluffy, add the
egg and continue beating until everything is well
amalgamated. Add the cold puréed carrots and mix in.

Sift the flour, baking powder, cinnamon and ginger on to
the mixture and mix until incorporated. Finally mix in the
coconut and papaya. Drop heaped teaspoons on to your
lined baking sheets, then flatten and squidge them into
thinnish circles with the back of a spoon. Bake for about
10 minutes until golden, then transfer to a wire rack to
cool. Delicious.

Mildon flapjacks

Flapjacks are just pushing the boundary of what is or what isn't a biscuit, but my reckoning is that you would eat them as you would a biscuit, so here they are. Thanks to my friend Helen who gave me her recipe. It's one where you get what, to my mind, is a proper flapjack – still slightly chewy and moist. Very comforting and the oats are amazingly good for you. We'll skip over the other ingredients' health benefits. But they must be good for your mental health. Surely...

✷ Makes 1 batch

250 g/9 oz/generous 1 cup butter, plus extra for greasing
250 g/9 oz/1¼ cups caster (superfine) sugar
175 g/6 oz/½ cup golden (corn) syrup
500 g/1 lb 2 oz/3¼ cups jumbo oats

Preheat the oven to 180°C/350°F/Gas Mark 4 and grease a 20 cm/8 inch square baking tin well (if it's a bit bigger or rectangular, please don't worry, just go for it).

Melt the butter, sugar and golden syrup in a large pan. When melted, add the oats and stir in, then tip the whole lot into the tin and press down firmly. Bake for about 25 minutes until pale golden. It may look slightly undercooked and very soft, but it sets as it cools. The key is not to overcook the flapjack, as this way it remains chewy. If you cook it too much, it will be harder. When the flapjack comes out of the oven, quickly score it into pieces with a sharp knife and leave to cool in the tin.

Sesame crackers

If you like sesame seeds, you will love these. If you don't like sesame seeds, leave them out and pop in a seed of your choice – hemp, poppy, flaxseed would all go well – just make sure you choose small seeds rather than something chunky like pumpkin. These crackers are lovely with cheese or dippy things like hummus. They also keep really well in an airtight tin.

✳ Makes 1 batch

150 g/5 oz/scant 1 cup whole-meal (whole-wheat) flour
150 g/5 oz/generous 1 cup plain white (all-purpose) flour, plus extra for dusting
1 tsp salt
1½ tsp baking powder
3 dessertspoons plain yoghurt
50 g/2 oz/4 tbsp butter
2 tbsp sesame seeds
Ice-cold water (optional)

Preheat the oven to 180°C/350°F/Gas Mark 4 and line 2 baking sheets with silicone liners.

Sift the flours, salt and baking powder into a large bowl. Add the yoghurt and mix in. Melt the butter in a pan then add the seeds and cook until they start to smell nutty. Add the butter mixture to the flour and stir in. Don't go straight in with your hands unless you want third-degree burns. When it's cool enough to handle, get your hands in and knead away. You may need a bit of iced water to help things along. Stop adding the water when you have a smooth and non-sticky dough.

Place the dough on a floured surface and knead away for a few minutes, then roll out as thin as you can, about 3 mm/⅛ inches or less. Cut out shapes and lay the biscuits on your lined baking sheets. Prod them many, many times with a fork then bake for 10 minutes until golden and crispy. Leave to cool.

Thyme and cheese biscuits

These are firmly in the 'savoury biscuit as snack' or pre-drink nibble category, rather than belonging to the cracker brigade. Very moreish and I haven't yet met anyone who didn't get quite greedy when they were handed around.

✳ Makes 1 batch

50 g/2 oz/4 tbsp butter, softened
115 g/4 oz/generous 1 cup grated
   strong Cheddar cheese
1 tsp English mustard powder
Pinch of salt
100 g/4 oz/¾ cup plain
   (all-purpose) flour
1 tsp dried thyme or 2 tsp fresh
   thyme, chopped

Blend the butter and cheese together in a bowl. If the butter is soft, this takes moments. Add everything else and mix to form a dough. Roll the dough into a thinnish log, about 2–3cm/¾–1¼ inches in diameter, depending on how large you want your biscuits, then wrap in cling film and chill in the refrigerator for at least 30 minutes. You can freeze it happily at this stage too.

Preheat the oven to 180°C/350°F/Gas Mark 4 and line 2 baking sheets with silicone liners.

Unwrap the dough and slice into 5 mm/¼ inch pieces, place on your lined baking sheets and bake for about 10 minutes until golden. Transfer to a wire rack to cool (or at least get to the warm stage), then place on a plate and make people happy.

Blue cheese and walnut biscuits

You know when you get an idea into your head and you can't let go of it? Well, that happened here. I thought that blue cheese and walnuts would go very well in a savoury biscuit, so set about making them. Several calamities and large quantities of Stilton later ... we have blue cheese and walnut biscuits. The ground rice gives them a lovely crunch and even those who aren't particularly partial to blue cheese will hoover these up. Hoorah!

✳ Makes 1 batch

110 g/4 oz/8 tbsp butter, softened
85 g/3½ oz Stilton or other firm
    blue cheese
60 g/2½ oz/¼ cup ground rice
100 g/4 oz/¾ cup self-raising
    (self-rising) flour, plus extra
    for dusting
30 g/1 oz/scant ⅓ cup walnuts,
    chopped
Pinch of paprika

Cream the butter and cheese together in a large bowl until fluffy, then simply add all the other ingredients and mix until you have a fairly sticky dough. Wrap the dough in cling film and leave to chill in the refrigerator for at least an hour.

Preheat the oven to 190°C/375°F/Gas Mark 5 and line 2 baking sheets with silicone liners.

Unwrap the dough and place on a floured surface. If it's still a bit sticky to roll, knead in a little more flour. Roll the dough out to about 4–5 mm/¼ inch thick and cut out shapes. Use small cutters as these biscuits are really rich. Place on your lined baking sheets and bake for about 15 minutes until mildly golden. Transfer to a wire rack to cool.

Cecilia's Parmesan biscuits

This recipe is yet another from the wonder-baker, Cecilia. Enough said. You know they'll be good.

✱ Makes 1 batch

150 g/5 oz/generous 1 cup plain (all-purpose) flour
110 g/4 oz Parmesan cheese, grated
1 tsp baking powder
Pinch of salt
Pinch of paprika
75 g/3 oz/6 tbsp butter, cubed
2 large free-range egg yolks

Mix all the dry ingredients together in a large bowl. Add the butter and rub it in with your fingertips until the mixture looks like fine breadcrumbs. Add the egg yolk and form the dough into a ball. Wrap the dough in cling film and leave to rest in the refrigerator for about 30 minutes.

Preheat the oven to 200°C/400°F/Gas Mark 6 and line 2 baking sheets with silicone liners.

Unwrap the dough and roll it out on a lightly floured surface to about 3 mm/⅛ inch thick. Cut out small shapes and place on your lined baking sheets. Bake for 8–10 minutes until golden and smelling like heaven. Leave to cool.

Index